THE FRENCH CHALLENGE

THE FRENCH CHALLENGE

Adapting to Globalization

Philip H. Gordon

and

Sophie Meunier

BROOKINGS INSTITUTION PRESS
Washington, D.C.

Copyright © 2001
THE BROOKINGS INSTITUTION
1775 Massachusetts Avenue, N.W., Washington, D.C. 20036
www.brookings.edu

Library of Congress Cataloging-in-Publication data

Gordon, Philip H., 1962–
  The French challenge : adapting to globalization / Philip H. Gordon
and Sophie Meunier.
    p. cm.
  Includes bibliographical references and index.
  ISBN 0-8157-0260-4 (cloth) — ISBN 0-8157-0261-2 (alk. paper)
  1. France—Foreign economic relations. 2. Globalization.
3. France—Economic conditions—1995–. 4. France—Politics
and government—1995–. I. Meunier, Sophie. II. Title.
  HF1543 .G67 2001
  337.44—dc21   2001004712

9 8 7 6 5 4 3 2 1

The paper used in this publication meets minimum requirements of the
American National Standard for Information Sciences—Permanence of
Paper for Printed Library Materials: ANSI Z39.48-1992.

Typeset in Sabon

Composition by AlphaWebTech
Mechanicsville, Maryland

Printed by R. R. Donnelley and Sons
Harrisonburg, Virginia

To

Rachel, Noah, Benjamin, and Dinah Gordon

and

Yacine, Idir, and Ines Ait-Sahalia

Foreword

The massive antiglobalization street protests at the July 2001 G-8 summit in Genoa—following similar demonstrations at other international gatherings in Gotenberg, Prague, Washington, Davos, and Seattle—have brought the globalization debate to the attention of citizens all around the world. Nowhere, however, has globalization received greater attention than in France, where political and business leaders, intellectuals, and the public at large have been debating the potential merits and dangers of a world in which people, capital, goods, and ideas travel across borders as never before. As Philip Gordon and Sophie Meunier argue in this book, most French people recognize that globalization can bring great economic benefits to their country, but at the same time they worry about its effect on income distribution, job security, France's culture, and its standing in the world. While globalization challenges all societies, the authors argue, it poses a particular challenge to France because of the country's statist political tradition, commitment to social equality, special attachment to language, culture and identity, and long-standing desire to provide an alternative model to that of the United States.

These challenges are behind the title of this book, which echoes that of Jean-Jacques Servan-Schreiber's 1967 bestseller, *Le défi américain* (*The American Challenge*). Servan-Schreiber described how evolving American business practices were challenging French and European economic traditions and sent a wake-up call to the French: adapt or disappear under the weight of American domination. Gordon and Meunier describe the different but related challenge of globalization (many elements of which are not so different from the trends that Servan-Schreiber was already seeing in the late 1960s), which calls for France to adapt its economic, political, and cultural practices to the modern world. While arguing that France is adapting its society and economy much more significantly and successfully than most observers realize, the authors also address the other "French challenge"—France's challenge to the rest of the world to respond to globalization in a way that tempers its more damaging effects. The French call this attempt to manage globalization *mondialisation maîtrisée,* and Gordon and Meunier show how French ideas can and cannot contribute to other countries' attempts to deal with the phenomenon.

The origin of this project can be traced back to the conference "France in Europe, Europe in France," held at Harvard University in December 1999—the same week as the now famous World Trade Organization meeting in Seattle. Gordon, who had just become the first director of the Brookings Center on the United States and France (CUSF), presented a paper on France's search for a new political role in the age of globalization. He also stressed the extraordinary adaptation of French business to economic globalization, which he has had the opportunity to observe over the years as a visiting professor at INSEAD, the international business school based outside Paris. Meunier, a French scholar specializing in European trade politics at Princeton University, gave a paper on the growing importance of the antiglobalization movement in France (symbolized by José Bové, the farmer who dismantled the construction site of a McDonald's outlet in France in August 1999) and examined why France was apparently resisting globalization more than were its European partners. Comparing notes, Gordon and Meunier realized that France seemed to be both loudly resisting globalization and quietly adapting to it at the same time and they decided to explore this apparent paradox in more detail; this volume is the result. Most existing writing on France and globalization (much of it in French) is highly polemical, either taking a strong, ideological stand against globalization or arguing—wrongly, in Gordon and Meunier's view—that France has completely failed to adapt to it. By contrast, in this book the authors present a thorough, careful look at the challenge of globalization for France, as well as at France's response to this challenge. As a result, it will be useful not only to those interested in contemporary developments on the French economic and political landscape, but more generally to all those interested in how advanced industrialized societies can cope with what is arguably the primary social, political, and economic challenge of the twenty-first century.

The authors would like to thank a number of people who read and commented on all or various parts of the manuscript at different stages, including Suzanne Berger, Alain Beuve-Méry, Antony Blinken, Frédéric Bozo, Laurent Burin des Roziers, Julius (Bill) Friend, Ellen Frost, Marion Fourcade-Gourinchas, David Gordon, Peter Hall, Stanley Hoffmann, Richard Kuisel, Michèle Lamont, Nick Lardy, Marc Leland, Dan Leeds, James Lindsay, James Lowenstein, Patrick Messerlin, Bernard Meunier, Jacques Mistral, Pascal Riché, Simon Serfaty, Jeremy Shapiro, James Steinberg, Gunnar Trumbull, Justin Vaïsse, and Dan Wicks. They are especially grateful to Bridget Alway, who provided first-rate research assistance on everything from stock options to cinema, with the able assistance of CUSF interns Lindsay Martin, Sean Kellman, and Josie Gabel. At the Brookings Institution Press, Tanjam Jacobson did her usual superb job of editing, Carlotta Ribar proofread the pages, and Robert Elwood provided the index. Todd DeLelle thoroughly fact-checked the manuscript.

The authors would also like to thank the German Marshall Fund of the United States for its support of this project.

Finally, and most important, the authors are also grateful for the support, indulgence, and great company of their families (themselves products of globalization): Rachel, Noah, Benjamin, and Dinah Gordon and Yacine, Idir, and Ines Ait-Sahalia.

The views expressed in this volume are those of the authors and should not be ascribed to any person or institution acknowledged above or to the trustees, officers, or other staff members of the Brookings Institution.

MICHAEL H. ARMACOST
President

October 2001
Washington, D.C.

Contents

THE FRENCH
CHALLENGE

CHAPTER ONE

How Globalization Challenges France

In August 1999 a forty-six-year-old sheep farmer named José Bové was arrested for dismantling the construction site of a new McDonald's restaurant in the southern French town of Millau. He acted, he argued, in protest against U.S. retaliatory trade sanctions against European products (notably, French cheese) and the uncontrolled spread of free market globalization. By attacking McDonald's, and getting himself photographed in handcuffs in the process, the publicity-conscious Bové was striking out at the symbol of U.S.-inspired globalization, a perceived threat to French identity and culinary traditions. A few months later Bové built on his fame by smuggling huge chunks of Roquefort cheese into Seattle, where he was among the leaders of the antiglobalization protests against the World Trade Organization summit in November.

Bové's crusade against globalization struck a chord in France. He became an instant media celebrity and was widely compared to Astérix the Gaul, the popular French cartoon character who led his tiny village in resistance against the Roman occupiers.[1] By blending culture and agriculture, trade and identity, resistance to American hegemony and the French tradition of popular rebellion, Bové came to symbolize a France that felt threatened by globalization. Public opinion surveys showed why his message was so popular. In a range of recent polls, 72 percent said they felt "suspicious" of globalization, 65 percent perceived it as a direct cause of a worsening of social inequality, 56 percent said it threatened French identity, and 55 percent saw it as a threat to French jobs and companies.[2] In a poll taken at the time of Bové's trial, in June 2000, 45 percent said they "supported" or "felt sympathy" for him (with only 4 percent "opposed" or "hostile"), and 51 percent said they agreed with his positions on economic and financial globalization (as against 28 percent who did not agree).[3] Large majorities (75 percent and 65 percent, respectively) said they agreed with Bové on the issues of defending small farms and avoiding *la malbouffe*—a neologism that conjures up the image of bad, processed, and unhealthy food.[4]

Bové's antics, and his unquestionable talent for attracting the attention of the worldwide media (ironically, taking advantage of one aspect of globalization itself), have helped provoke a debate both within France and beyond about the pros and cons of a world in which financial, commercial, human, cultural, and technology flows are faster and more extensive than ever before. In France, this actually began in the early 1990s as a debate about European integration (which also meant ever freer movements of capital, goods, and people). By the end of the decade, however, globalization had become the omnipresent topic—spurred on by some much publicized factory closings by multinational companies in France; the debate over new technologies, such as the Internet, and new sciences, such as biotechnology; World Trade Organization (WTO) rulings allowing sanctions against traditional French products like cheese and foie gras; and the spread of "mad cow" and foot and mouth diseases from the United Kingdom. French bookstores have in recent years become filled with (most often critical) titles about globalization, including Viviane Forrester's bestsellers *The Economic Horror* (which sold 350,000 copies in France) and *A Strange Dictatorship* and Bové's *The World Is Not for Sale*.[5] French television regularly airs programs with titles like "Globalization: The Counter-Attack," "The Other Globalization," and "Globalization: Yes or No?"[6] The French daily *Le Monde* published 2,375 separate articles with references to "globalization" during 1999 and 2000 (as compared with 705 in the *New York Times* during the same period), and French president Jacques Chirac has given no fewer than 163 speeches on globalization since his mandate began in 1995.[7] References to France and globalization in the European press also grew exponentially during the 1990s, rising from just one in 1990 to sixteen in 1995, 384 in 1999, and 451 in 2000.[8] Numerous French intellectuals, politicians, and interest groups have joined a national debate about the effects of globalization, cultural uniformity, and Americanization, helping to force the issue onto the public agenda and shaping the image of France around the world.[9]

Not surprisingly, in a country where people traditionally look to the state for guidance and protection, French politicians have felt obliged to address globalization in their political programs and pronouncements. While only the extremes of the political spectrum have called for the process (somehow) to be halted, mainstream politicians from the Left and the Right have argued for measures to regulate and temper some of its perverse effects. Both socialist prime minister Lionel Jospin and conservative president Chirac often speak of the need for alternatives to unregulated markets of goods, money, and people and demand more "rules" to govern globalization. Jospin, even as he continues to liberalize and privatize large sections of the French economy (or perhaps, to create some needed political cover *because* he is doing so), has not abandoned his party's traditionally left-wing discourse on the necessity of "controlling market forces [and] combating the excesses of liberalism," while denouncing "the dangers of unbridled globalization driven by jungle capitalism."[10] Chirac, while on the political Right, was in fact elected in 1995 on a platform stressing the state's role in ensuring social protection and help for the least advantaged members of society. He, too, warns against uncontrolled markets and has complained about the sacrifices French workers must make "to safeguard the investment benefits of Scottish widows and California pensioners."[11] Chirac is also a strong advocate of international agreements to manage the geopolitical effects of globalization and insists on the need to preserve France's unique role in a world dominated by the chief proponent of globalization, the United States.[12] Finally, practically all French leaders agree on the need for measures to preserve cultural diversity in the face of globalization's harmonizing influences. "Cultural uniformity," Foreign Minister Hubert Védrine has made clear, is something that France "cannot accept."[13]

The Bové phenomenon, together with the public opinion numbers, political rhetoric, and media discussion, might make it seem fair to conclude that France is experiencing a backlash against globalization and even taking the lead in a growing international movement to slow or contain it.[14]

To an extent this is true. As this book shows, the French really do worry about the effects of globalization on their society, economy, and culture and they are receptive to proposals to regulate the phenomenon.

But this is only half, and perhaps the least interesting half, of the story. The full story about France and globalization is that the very phenomenon that is causing so much anxiety among the French is at the same time profoundly transforming France's economy, society, and political system, often in very positive ways. For the apparent paradox at the heart of this book is that France is resisting globalization (sometimes loudly) and adapting to it (far more than most people realize) at the same time.

The greatest example of globalization's impact on France, and of France's adaptation, is in the economic domain. The nature of the French economy has changed radically over the past two decades, and especially in the past few years. Breaking with its mercantilist and *dirigiste* past, France has since the early 1980s converted to market liberalization, both as the necessary by-product of European integration and globalization and as a result of deliberate efforts by policymakers. For example, whereas the French state used to own large sectors of the economy partly to keep them out of foreign control, a Socialist-led left-wing government coalition is now proceeding with privatization, allowing foreign companies to purchase large or even majority shares in formerly state-owned companies. Prime Minister Lionel Jospin may prefer the euphemism "private sector participation," but the reality is that his government has sold off more state-owned assets than the previous six governments put together. Communist transport minister Jean-Claude Gayssot's announcement of a partial sell-off of Air France in February 1998 was a telling symbol of how much France has changed. Whereas fifteen years ago foreign ownership of French firms was only around 10 percent, today over 40 percent of the shares on the French bourse are held abroad, and foreigners own more than half of key French companies such as Société Générale, Alcatel, and Suez.[15] Trade—exports plus imports—as a share of French GDP has increased from just 24.9 percent in 1962 to a record 49.4 percent in 1997, as high as for Germany (49 percent) and twice as high as for the United States (25 percent) and Japan (21 percent).[16]

Evidence of globalization in the French economy is even more striking when one looks at the way particular French companies are taking advantage of new international opportunities, largely through a wave of international mergers and acquisitions over which the once all-powerful state has had little influence. Just to take one prominent example, on the same day in June 2000 that France's Publicis bought the famed British advertising firm Saatchi and Saatchi, Paris-based Vivendi completed its $34 billion purchase of Seagram's, the Canadian liquor company that also owned U.S.-based Universal Studios and Polygram Records. The idea of a major Hollywood studio being owned by Vivendi, once a local French water company, is perhaps as important a symbol of the new France's adaptation to globalization as is the mustachioed Bové and his Roquefort. Many leading French companies, like Michelin, Alcatel, and Axa, make three-quarters or more of their profits abroad.[17]

Moreover, France's adaptation to the globalizing world economy is finally paying off in terms of economic performance. French economic growth has been positive since 1993 and has averaged above 3 percent for the past three years—the best performance of all the large European economies and the best growth in France for more than a decade.[18] The budget deficit has fallen to less than 2 percent, helping to lower the national debt–GDP ratio to under 60 percent and bring short- and long-term interest rates down to historic lows of 2.9 percent and 4.6 percent, respectively.[19] The stock market, buoyed by the inflow of capital from abroad, rose by 51 percent in 1999, and in 2000, while nearly all other major European and North American markets were tumbling, held its ground.[20] The trade balance has been in surplus for five of the past six years (the exception being 2000, because of rising energy prices), and inflation is practically nonexistent. Perhaps most important, unemployment—the blight on French economic performance for nearly thirty years—has fallen to single digits (8.7 percent) for the first time in a decade, with the creation of more than 500,000 new jobs in 2000, the greatest percentage gain in jobs since 1970 and the most ever in a single year.[21] France thus began the new century in a more favorable economic situation than it had seen for more than thirty years.[22]

A Working Definition of Globalization

What, precisely, do we mean by "globalization," and what do the French mean by it? In this book, globalization refers to the increasing speed, ease, and extent with which capital, goods, services, technologies, people, cultures, information, and ideas now cross borders. Some have questioned whether there is really anything new in all of this, and they are right to point out both that the globe has been "shrinking" for centuries and that earlier periods—for example, from the 1880s to the 1910s—also saw great increases in international human and economic exchange.[23] But the acceleration of the phenomenon over the past two decades, and in particular since the early 1990s, has been undeniable, as are the differences with earlier such eras.

As Thomas L. Friedman and many others have pointed out, whereas trade and investment as shares of GDP may not be at much higher levels than they were at the end of the nineteenth century for certain countries, the degree, intensity, speed, volume, and geographic reach of globalization today far exceeds anything that has come before.[24] Today's globalization can be measured by the $1.5 trillion that moves around the world electronically every day; the nearly $1 trillion of foreign direct investments that were made in 1999; the annual international trade flows of some $7 trillion; the $720 billion of global mergers and acquisitions for 1999; the existence of 63,000 transnational companies with 690,000 foreign affiliates; the 3 million people who cross international borders every day; the more than 100 billion minutes spent on international phone connections during 2000; and the 250 million people around the world who have access to the Internet.[25] All this interaction ties the world together and opens societies and economies up to foreign influences in unprecedented ways.

This openness, as is often pointed out, is due in large part to technological advances over the past few decades, and particularly in recent years.[26] As a result, the costs of international shipping, transportation, travel, communication, and financial interaction have all fallen, in some cases dramatically. But it is important to remember that globalization has also been driven by changes in ideas, and therefore policies. As recently as twenty years ago, much of the world—the Soviet Union, all of Eastern Europe, China, India, Southeast Asia, Africa, the Middle East, and most of Latin America—was either largely cut off from the international economy or at least highly reluctant to open borders to trade, capital, and information flows. Even in Western Europe, not all governments were yet persuaded of the beneficial effects of free trade, capital and investment flows. Today, however, while there is still a range of views on the best way to implement modern capitalism, the thinking about international openness is dramatically different. Not only has the European Union completed its single market and ended all restrictions on capital flows (no longer opposed even by governments of the Left), but leaders of huge parts of the international economy—China, Southeast Asia, Latin America, Eastern Europe, and Russia—are now convinced that openness to trade and foreign investment are in the best interests of their countries. While there is no guarantee that this trend will go on forever—previous periods of economic openness, after all, have been reversed—there is no doubt that it has already progressed quite a long way, and few signs that it is running out of steam.

It is important to keep in mind that "globalization" actually encompasses many distinct, if related, developments, not all of which are driven by the same forces or proceed (or recede) at the same pace. As Robert Keohane and Joseph Nye have pointed out, it has distinct economic, military, environmental, social, cultural, and political components.[27] They note, for example, that economic globalization progressed between 1850 and 1914 but receded between 1914 and 1945, while many aspects of military and social globalization progressed between 1914 and 1945.[28] Similarly, the effects of the different strands of globalization can vary considerably: economic globalization might force once-protected industries to compete or affect the relative return on labor or capital; informational globalization (via the Internet, for example) might undermine the control of authoritarian governments; military globalization (the growing ability to project forces and military power around the world) might enhance the global influence of the United States; and environmental globalization might make populations more vulnerable to disease, pollution, or other environmental issues that originate beyond their own borders.

In the chapters that follow, we try to keep these distinctions in mind and make clear in each case which aspects of this wide-ranging phenomenon are relevant to the discussion. At the same time, particularly when discussing French reactions to globalization, one must recognize that most people do not distinguish among these various elements and often think of globalization as a single phenomenon that cannot be accepted or rejected in part. Many of the different strands of globalization do, in fact, come bundled together. Thus we try to balance the need to disaggregate a complex phenomenon with the need to see globalization as a package of closely related developments that cannot be discussed in isolation from one another.

Finally, it is impossible to discuss the way globalization affects France and the way the French react to globalization without noting the equation made by many in France between "globalization" and "Americanization." To be sure, there are many products, both good and bad, of globalization in France—sushi, "reality television," low-priced manufactured imports, mad cow and foot and mouth diseases, and intra-European foreign direct investment, to name just a few—that have nothing to do with the United

States. In this sense, the equation is highly misleading. Yet it is also true that globalization often comes with an American face—because of the role of the English language in global culture and business, the size of the U.S. economy and its large share of world trade and investment, Americans' comfort with the liberal economic practices associated with economic globalization, and the United States' unique power to project military force and diplomatic influence abroad. This is one of the reasons why globalization poses particular problems to France, which has long competed with the United States for world influence and, like the United States, has always seen itself as something of a model for the rest of the world. These are important factors to keep in mind in assessing the French reaction to globalization.

Why Globalization Is a Particular Challenge for France

France is hardly the only country where globalization has become both a political and a public issue. Particularly since the WTO debacle in Seattle (followed a few months later by further protests at the January 2000 meeting of the world's leading industrialists at the World Economic Forum in Davos, Switzerland), consumer groups, environmentalists, and human rights activists all around the world have brought attention to the dangers of unchecked globalization—such as the undemocratic nature of the trade regime, the social failures of the free market, and the real risks of environmental degradation. From the United States to Japan, from Brazil to India, substantial sections of public opinion and key government leaders are now seriously questioning the effects of globalization and looking for ways to control it.

Yet if globalization is now an issue everywhere, it is a particular challenge for France for several reasons. First, it directly challenges the country's statist, *dirigiste* political and economic tradition because of the degree to which it requires abandoning state control over the economy—and thereby over society. As we show in chapter 2, the French economy has evolved significantly away from *dirigisme* over the past twenty years, but the process has been slow and painful and it is far from complete. Today the French still have one of the largest state sectors in Europe and they still look to the state, rather than the market, to ensure their well-being. Despite great efforts over the past few years to trim the role of the state in the economy, government expenditure still stands at 54 percent of France's GDP, a historic peak and significantly higher than in most industrialized countries. Nearly 25 percent of French workers get their paychecks from the state (compared with an average of 17 percent in the Eurozone and 15 percent in the United States).[29] All this makes it particularly difficult for the French to accept that their economic, social, and cultural fate is controlled less and less by Paris and more and more by the rest of the world. It also helps explain another phenomenon apparent in this study, the fact that France is actually adapting to the globalized world economy to a far greater degree than French leaders—who must maintain the notion that the French state is still in control—are prepared to admit.

The second reason globalization is so difficult for France is that the French are strongly attached to their culture and identity, and many feel that these are now threatened by a globalization that they equate with Americanization. This is, of course, an old theme, going all the way back to the interwar period, when French writers first started to criticize U.S. mass culture, conformity, and emphasis on material wealth. It emerged strongly again in the postwar period as the American role in Europe grew and French people on the Right and the Left worried about "coca-colonization" (a reference to the aggressively marketed American soft drink's domination in France) and the "American challenge," the title of a bestselling book about the domination of American companies in Europe.[30] It has reemerged and taken on particular momentum today, however, because of the way in which new technologies and the growing ideology of free trade have helped to make societies more susceptible than ever to foreign cultural influences, and in particular to the cultural influence of the United States. The spread of the Internet and other communications technologies; trade liberalization in agricultural goods, intellectual property, and services; and the dominant role of the United States (and thus the English language) in global business all combine to make the French fear for their cultural, linguistic, culinary traditions—in short, their national identity—in a globalizing world. It was no coincidence that the publicity-conscious Bové chose McDonald's as the target for his protests.

Third, globalization challenges some of the most fundamental principles and values on which the French republic was built. Whereas the French republic is based, in theory, on rationality—the enlightened state engaged in the improvement of the collective destiny of the French people—globalization is inevitably a messy and disorderly process that interferes with the state's ability to play that role. The United States, proud of its tradition of individualism and with a population deeply skeptical of government, thrives in such a chaotic world and willingly accepts the combination of great successes and inequalities that globalization creates. France, however, is uncomfortable with such a direct challenge to the notions of *égalité* and *fraternité* that, for a population that has seen its share of divisions over the centuries, are more than just slogans.[31]

The fourth reason globalization is a particular challenge for France is because it is seen to threaten the global stature and role of a country that has long prided itself on its international prominence. Whereas smaller European countries largely abandoned global geopolitics after World War II (and larger ones, like Britain, felt they could best maintain their global roles by working closely with the United States), France has never given up its desire for global influence in its own right.[32] Globalization threatens this influence, however, by reinforcing the dominance of the country that most stands in the way of France's quest for diplomatic influence: the United States. Not surprisingly, in a European public opinion survey that asked what the word *globalization* first brought to mind, the top French response was "U.S. dominance"—25 percent, compared with only 8 perent in Italy, 6 percent in Britain, and just 3 percent in Germany.[33] To the extent that globalization means ceding world leadership to the United States—or even limiting the country's traditional diplomatic role by ceding more power to collective organizations like the European Union or the United Nations—it is particularly difficult for France to accept.

Finally, it is probably fair to say that many in France resist globalization because they can afford to do so. Arguably, the British in the late 1970s, and to a lesser degree the Americans in the early 1980s, were willing to turn to economic neoliberalism (with the elections of Margaret Thatcher and Ronald Reagan) not only because of their more liberal political traditions but also because of the perception that their economic performance had declined so much that fundamental change was necessary. The French, however, for all their problems with inflation, and especially unemployment, never became so disgruntled with their relative reliance on the state that they were willing to abandon it, and the incentive to do so has diminished even further with the economic successes of the past several years. As French writer and analyst Dominique Moïsi put it in 1998, "France's struggle with globalization is complicated by its people's high quality of life. Most of the French feel they have little to gain and much to lose from globalization—the space and beautiful diversity of their countryside, the quality of their food and wine, and the respect for tradition. Why risk all these unique pleasures for the sake of an uncertain competition in a global world? The temptation for many Frenchmen is to retreat into the protective bubble of the good life."[34]

French foreign minister Hubert Védrine has summed up globalization's challenge to France by candidly (and euphemistically) admitting that "globalization does not *automatically* benefit France." This, he explains, is because it "develops according to principles that correspond neither to French tradition nor French culture," including free market economics, mistrust of the state, common law, the English language, individualism inconsistent with the republican tradition, and the reinforcement of the role of the United States. "France," he concludes, "must thus make an exceptional effort to adapt."[35]

This book is about this effort to adapt and its consequences. We analyze the impact that globalization is having on France's economy, cultural identity, domestic politics, and foreign relations, and conclude with an assessment of France's response to the challenge of globalization—its efforts to manage and control it.

Chapter 2 explores the structural transformation of the French economy, driven first by liberalization within the European Union and more recently by globalization. We explain the *dirigiste* roots of French economic policy and then show how French economic policy has changed considerably since François Mitterrand finally accepted the constraints of the global market in 1983. By examining a wide variety of possible measures of acceptance to globalization and liberalization—privatization, the development of the stock market, the globalization of industry, economic openness and trade policy, monetary and exchange rate policy, taxation, labor regulations, and the integration of technology—we conclude that the French economy's adaptation to globalization has been far reaching and largely successful, even if French leaders prefer to downplay the extent of these changes because public opinion remains skeptical of liberalism and wedded to a strong state. We call this adaptation "globalization by stealth."

If the French are (reluctantly) embracing the economic aspects of globalization, they have real concerns about its impact on their culture and identity. Chapter 3 looks at the relationship between trade, culture, and identity and explains why globalization has rendered the three inseparable. We argue that the link between trade, culture, and identity has become more explicit than it was in previous decades, when trade in "regular" goods was clearly distinct from trade in "cultural" goods, and explain why France is particularly receptive to arguments that it must defend its cultural, linguistic, and culinary traditions. French fears for this proud cultural heritage are exaggerated, however, and many of the methods chosen to preserve it are futile or counterproductive. France has a strong and attractive culture that will not disappear. On the contrary, while globalization in part "threatens" French culture, it also offers new opportunities for speading it around the world (*rayonnement*).

Chapter 4 discusses how globalization is reshaping French domestic politics. In particular, we examine how globalization is contributing to the restructuring of the traditional French political spectrum and blurring the traditional differences between Left and Right. We argue that while globalization is unlikely to lead to the formation of new parties or alignments, it is nonetheless making an important informal impact by imposing new dividing lines, often with the result that the extremes of the political spectrum have more in common with each other than with their more traditional allies. Former hard-line conservative interior minister Charles Pasqua's sympathy for Leftist radical Bové's antiglobalization campaign is just one example of this phenomenon. We also examine the range of public opinion and political attitudes toward globalization and explore the effects of the antiglobalization movement on the traditional parties and their platforms. We show how even leaders who are doing much to adapt France to globalization, such as Jospin, are constrained in their ability to admit it, because of the antiglobalization movement and the French public's general attachment to the notion of an activist state.

Chapter 5 explores France's efforts to "manage" or "tame" globalization (what the French call *maîtriser la mondialisation*), and the possible consequences of the French stance for the rest of the world. We show how France uses a variety of tools—the maintenance of a welfare state, the construction of a strong Europe, trade policy, international financial reform, and foreign policy—to soften the edges of the phenomenon of globalization. The French challenge is thus one of preserving the country's identity, heritage, and distinctiveness, while at the same time moving forward with the necessary adaptation to the requirements of a new economy and an interdependent world.

CHAPTER TWO

The New French Economy: Globalization by Stealth

"Le capitalisme de papa, c'est fini."
Michel Pébereau, chairman, Banque Nationale de Paris

The traditional view of the French economy—antiliberal, heavily state centered, antiglobalization, and inflexible—is gradually becoming outdated. To be sure, many aspects of the traditionally *dirigiste* state live on in France. Tax rates and government spending are among the highest in the world. The state still employs nearly one-quarter of all French workers. There are few prominent neoliberal thinkers and politicians in a country where the notion of "economic liberalism" is still highly suspect. The French education system perpetuates a tight circle of powerful elites who permeate industry and government, and therefore uphold the central role of the state. The traditional characteristics of a national economy do not change overnight, and they certainly have not done so in France.

But the real story of the French economy of the past twenty years is not so much how the state has maintained its traditional grip, but rather how the country has gradually, and quietly, adapted to the requirements of the emerging global, liberal economy. The driving forces of this change have been the related processes of Europeanization and economic globalization, both of which require the state to reduce its role in economic life and allow the market to work. Indeed, by any measure—privatization, the role of the stock market, the globalization of French industry, openness to trade, exchange rate policy, taxation, labor relations, or adoption of technology—it is apparent that France has steadily, if reluctantly, liberalized its economy and opened it up to international competition and influence.

The transformation of the French economy has happened quietly, because it remains taboo to sing too loudly the praises of liberalization and globalization. The French still look back proudly at the role of state planning and intervention in creating such a prosperous and attractive country with generous social protection, and they remain wary of the neoliberal doctrines that have been embraced—not only by the political Right—in the United States and Great Britain. In France, even today, it is more politically popular and socially acceptable to denounce the ravages of "jungle capitalism" or the "dictatorship of stockholders," to use Prime Minister Lionel Jospin's words, than it is to praise the free market.[1] Yet while they call for the state to mitigate capitalism's negative side effects, France's political leaders—and even more its business community—have come to realize that it is no longer possible for the state to play a dominant role in running the economy, in a European single market and a globalizing world. The result has been a gradual, if rather quiet, freeing of the French economy from state control: "globalization by stealth."

The adoption of a new French model seems to be paying off. Whereas the first fifteen years after the 1983 U-turn—when France made the critical decision to free its economy, reduce the role of the state, and embrace fiscal and monetary discipline—were painful, the French economy has begun to prosper in the past few years. As late as the mid-1990s, with unemployment still at double-digit levels and growth stagnant, the French economy was still seen as one of Europe's laggards, and the most common words used to describe the French mood were *"malaise"* and *"morosité."*[2] Since then, however, growth has picked up markedly, unemployment is falling rapidly, and productivity is rising. As of July 2000, consumer confidence was at its highest level since the index was created in 1987, and instead of *malaise* analysts began writing about "optimistic France" and "the end of crisis."[3] The notion of a dynamic France as an economic motor of Europe, pulling even Germany along, might have seemed absurd a decade ago, but it is no longer so far-fetched.[4]

This chapter examines how globalization has forced the once *dirigiste* French state to adapt, primarily by liberalizing and opening up its economy in ways that would have seemed inconceivable as recently as twenty years ago. While many vestiges of *dirigisme* are still strong, and an often skeptical if not downright hostile public makes continued reform difficult and slow, the overall story is one of a country adapting in its own way to the requirements of an integrated world economy.

The *Dirigiste* Model

The traditional French economic model, known as *dirigisme*, appears antithetical to the economic liberalism of globalization. In the *dirigiste* model, the state has an important role to play in guiding national economic developments because it alone can identify and pursue the common interest, which is superior to the sum of private interests.[5] In the *dirigiste* model, the market is allowed to work, but only under the close supervision of the state, which controls many of its most important levers through extensive ownership of the means of production and finance, high taxation and spending, interventionist industrial policies, and close ties with the corporate world. This tradition goes back to King Louis XIV and his famed finance minister, Jean-Baptiste Colbert, who has given his name to a policy of protectionism and interventionism. It was deepened by strong Jacobin leaders like Napoléon, who (much as did General Charles de Gaulle 150 years later) sought to use the state's influence over the economy to enhance its political and military power.[6]

Yet the historic tradition of a predominant state role in the French economy is often exaggerated. In fact, Colbert and Napoléon notwithstanding, the development of genuinely state-led capitalism was primarily a twentieth century phenomenon and did not reach its peak until the 1960s. The first, albeit very limited, steps toward *dirigisme* were taken by the 1936 Popular Front coalition, which nationalized most of the French arms industry, the railways, and the Bank of France as a means of redistributing income and curbing the power of the "200 families" that allegedly controlled the country. But it was World War II—as elsewhere in Europe, and to a lesser degree in the United States—that greatly enhanced the state's involvement in economic affairs, primarily to deal with the shortages, bottlenecks, and need for social protection that inevitably resulted from six years of armed conflict. Just as important was the feeling among many French, on both the Right and the Left, that the unbridled capitalism that prevailed in Europe in the 1920s and 1930s had failed, leading only to Depression and war. At the end of the war, de Gaulle and those around him in the Provisional Government believed that an intelligent and activist state would be more efficient at organizing the economy than the market. Most of them also believed that social equality, prestige industries, traditional sectors (like agriculture and culture), and a strong national defense were just as important as economic growth per se.

At the heart of postwar *dirigisme* was the belief that the state could generate growth and modernize France through planning and industrial policy. In order to coordinate the economy, in 1946 de Gaulle set up a Planning Commission, headed by Jean Monnet, which reported directly to the prime minister. De Gaulle nationalized the banks; Air France; the gas, electricity, and coal industries; and most insurance firms. He also set up the Ecole nationale d'administration (ENA), which along with other *grandes écoles* would provide much of the leadership of France's nationalized industries (and many private ones, as well). Through planning, the *dirigiste* state brought together business leaders, trade unionists, experts and civil servants to discuss key industrial sectors and potential problem areas within the economy.[7] In later years, planning was used to launch the *"grands projets"* (major industrial initiatives) and support the creation of "national champions," large state-owned firms capable of standing up to international competition and bringing national prestige.[8]

The role of planning in France should not be exaggerated. The successive four-year plans largely provided guidance on where the economy should go, not heavy-handed commands of what to produce. Moreover France's membership in the European Economic Community from 1958 led to the rapid reduction of tariffs and a growing openness to European— and global—competition throughout the 1960s, including under de Gaulle. Still, the state's role in the economy grew steadily. In 1960 French government spending was still only 34.6 percent of GDP, but it would rise to 54.7 of GDP by 1996 (compared with 35 percent for the United States), one of the highest rates in the world.[9] As shown in figure 2-1, France's overall tax burden (including social charges) has also been among the highest in Europe, reaching over 30 percent of GDP by 1960, 40 percent by 1980, and over 45 percent in 2000.[10]

The postwar period was one of unprecedented growth, with GDP increasing by an average of 5.5 percent a year between 1958 and 1973.[11] Because the 1950s and 1960s also saw a large increase in state benefits, like social security and generous health care and pension benefits, many French people remember *dirigisme* fondly (often attributing to it more importance than it deserved). This favorable judgment—in contrast, for

Figure 2-1.   *Overall Tax Burden, Including Social Charges,*
1960–2001[a]

Percent of GDP

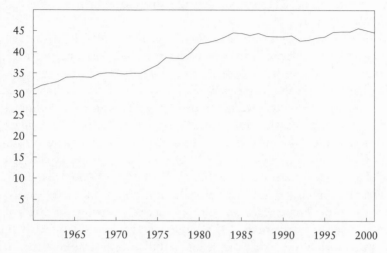

Source: Le Monde, *Bilan du Monde 2001* (Paris, 2001), p. 142.
a. Figures for 2000 and 2001 are estimates.

example, to Great Britain, where many people had judged their interventionist state a failure by the 1980s—would later contribute to France's
difficulty in adapting to the requirements of globalization. Why, many
French people felt (and continue to feel), fix something that is not fundamentally broken?

Over time, even the indicative role of the four-year plan diminished, its
importance eroded by economic recovery and ever more by open competition in the European Economic Community, making it harder for the
French state to control the levers of the economy. In 1974, the French
elected the first non-Gaullist president of the Fifth Republic, Valéry Giscard
d'Estaing, who came from the Orléaniste wing of France's political spectrum, the closest thing France has to a liberal movement.[12] Giscard's in-
stinct was to open the French economy further, but the effects of the
1973–74 oil crisis—rising prices, global recession, and growing unemployment in France—made that difficult, especially since the French now expected the state to protect them from the vicissitudes of the world economy.
Giscard attempted a policy of *"rigueur"* (austerity) in 1974 to squeeze out
inflation as the Germans were doing, but in 1975 he was persuaded by his

prime minister, Jacques Chirac, to seek rapid growth. This worked temporarily, but it soon led to a pattern all too familiar in the postwar French economy: accelerating inflation (which rose to nearly 10 percent in 1976), an overvalued franc, a large trade deficit, rising unemployment, and consequently, devaluation.[13]

With the failure of his economic plan, Chirac abruptly left government in 1976 and was replaced by the economist Raymond Barre. Barre quickly set France on a more classical liberal course: tightening monetary policy, increasing taxes, defending the franc vis-à-vis the deutsche mark, relaxing price controls, gradually lowering trade barriers, cutting aid to failing industries, offering incentives for public share ownership, and reducing the state's role in the economy overall. Indeed, the Barre Plan was the precursor to the economic model that after 1983 would form the basic paradigm for all French governments, of the Right or the Left, and would help ready the French economy to deal with globalization. But while Barre's heavy demands on the French had some initial success, allowing the Right to preserve a bare majority in the 1978 parliamentary elections, the 1979 oil crisis intervened, driving prices up again, re-inflating the trade deficit, and creating more unemployment. The French were not yet ready to believe that the state could not, or should not, protect them from the ravages of the global economy. In 1981 they threw out Giscard—and the Barre Plan with him. In their place the French elected a Socialist-Communist coalition that promised to break with capitalism and restore the country's economic health by using the very tool that Giscard and Barre had shunned: an interventionist state.

Mitterrand Meets Globalization

The 1981 election of François Mitterrand as president of the republic initially brought back *dirigisme* with a vengeance. Whereas Giscard's and Barre's policies were premised on the need to adapt to outside constraints— the oil crisis, the European Monetary System (EMS), and the global recession brought about by high interest rates in the United States—Mitterrand and his team believed France could escape these constraints by resorting to a familiar asset: the French state. The Mitterrand experiment, in other words, was an early rejection of the logic of what would later be called globalization. France, the new team believed, could save its own economy from the problems created by the rest of the world by taking control:

nationalizing banks and industries, loosening monetary policy, boosting spending, and redistributing wealth.

Once elected on such a platform, Mitterrand quickly moved forward with one of the most actively interventionist policies France had ever seen. In his first year in office, the government nationalized thirty-eight banks (including the large investment banks Paribas and Suez) and six major companies (including the chemicals firm Rhône-Poulenc, glassmaker Saint-Gobain, aluminum firm Péchiney, and the electronics company Thomson), at a cost of some 40 billion francs.[14] It raised the minimum wage by 15 percent between May 1981 and December 1982, raised family allowances (state aid to families with children) by up to 81 percent, increased housing allocations for low-income workers by 25 percent, and cut the working week from forty to thirty-nine hours, without corresponding reductions in pay.[15] In Mitterrand's first year government spending rose by 2.6 percent, and the state's share in industrial production rose from 15 percent to more than 30 percent.[16] The budget deficit rose from 0.4 percent of GDP in 1981 to 3 percent in 1982.

The international reaction was a harsh lesson for France. Because France was now far more dependent on international trade than previously (the share of imports and exports in French GDP had risen from less than 25 percent in the late 1950s to nearly 45 percent in 1983), domestic expansion at a time of global recession hurt French industry and led to a mounting trade deficit, which nearly doubled from 1981 to 1982.[17] The French stock market consequently dropped by 30 percent, the franc came under intense pressure, inflation remained near 10 percent, and by November 1981 the government had to announce a "pause" in the reforms (the same word that Léon Blum had used in 1936 to signal the end of the Popular Front's reforms). Germany, always cautious to avoid a break with France, was willing to allow the devaluation of the franc and the revaluation of the mark in October 1981 and June 1982. But the limits even of German tolerance were approaching, and with France running out of reserves, Bonn hinted that further revaluations would be conditional on a change in economic policy in Paris.

By early 1983, it was clear that the Mitterrand experiment could not escape the constraints of the world economy. Overcoming the arguments of some of his advisers, who wanted to break with Europe and pursue the autarkic approach at any cost, Mitterrand finally conceded that France had no choice but to uphold its commitment to the EMS, even if this meant devaluing the franc, cutting spending, and raising taxes and interest rates to defend the currency and halt runaway inflation.[18] It was the end of the *dirigiste* revival and the beginning of a long and gradual acceptance of the requirements of international economic openness and liberalism.

In 1984 Mitterrand installed a new team, headed by thirty-seven-year-old Laurent Fabius as prime minister. They largely succeeded in curbing the worst excesses of Mitterrand's first two years: by 1985 inflation was down to 5 percent, the trade deficit fell to 20 billion francs, and the franc was maintaining its value. By the following year, the economy was growing by 2.5 percent, the highest growth since Mitterrand had come to power, and the stock market had begun to rise.

The Mitterrand U-turn thus played an important role not only in France's adaptation to international economic integration but in the globalization story more generally. The Socialist experiment showed, to the French and to the rest of the world, that by the early 1980s, the thought of going it alone was no longer an option for a national economy—particularly one that was integrated into the European Community. Although Giscard and Barre had realized this by the late 1970s, the notion was controversial enough in France that their message would not prevail until, ironically, the Socialist François Mitterrand proved it to be true.

The New French Capitalism

Mitterrand had learned, painfully, that France was too deeply enmeshed in the integrating European and world economies to practice state-led capitalism along traditional lines. The following twenty years would see a deepening of global integration far surpassing anything France had ever experienced in the past. In part, this was the result of new thinking about how to achieve economic success, which led France to accept the Single European Act (completing the EU single market), abandon restrictions on capital flows, and continue to accept the constraints of the European Monetary System. In other ways, economic integration just happened: the rise of emerging markets, in which French companies were forced to compete; developments in information technology and the Internet, which enabled companies to gather information, market, and compete on a global level and investors to transfer funds quickly and inexpensively anywhere in the world; and dramatic reductions in the cost of global communication and transport. If France wanted to maintain its place as one of the world's leading economies, it would have to dramatically change the way it did business.

While it would be an exaggeration to suggest that France has completely abandoned *dirigisme* and that the legacy of the state-led approach has disappeared, the fact that the current economic changes discussed below are taking place under a left-wing government is an indication of how much the country's economic landscape has changed. In a country known for its deep, ideological divisions, the differences between Left and Right on the economy since the Mitterrand U-turn (in practice, if not in rhetoric) have been minimal. Notwithstanding the frequent turnover of government—the parliamentary majority swung to the Right in 1986, to the Left in 1988, to the Right in 1993, and to the Left in 1997, while the presidency shifted from Left to Right in 1995—economic management since 1983 has been driven more than anything by the need to adapt the French economy to the requirements of the European and global markets.

Privatization

Perhaps the most telling sign of France's acceptance that the market should play a greater role in the economy and the state a lesser role has been its willingness to put industrial management in private hands—and when necessary, foreign private hands. The past fifteen years have seen a massive retreat from public sector ownership of the economy: from a peak of 10.4 percent in 1985, the state's share has fallen to its prewar level of 5 percent.[19]

The biggest step along this road was the 200 billion franc privatization initiative of Prime Minister Jacques Chirac from 1986 to 1988, which reversed not only Mitterrand's 1981 nationalization program but also some of the bank nationalizion of de Gaulle in 1945. The sell-off included glassmaker Saint-Gobain, the television network TF1, the advertising firm Havas, and the defense manufacturer Matra. The momentum behind privatization was slowed by the 1987 stock market crash, and then by the Socialists' return to power from 1988 to 1993, when Mitterrand instead called for a policy of "*ni . . . ni . . .*"—neither privatization nor nationalization. But when the Right returned to power in 1993, Prime Ministers Edouard Balladur (1993–95) and Alain Juppé (1995–97) moved ahead to finish what Chirac had started. They sold Rhône Poulenc, Elf-Aquitaine, Total, BNP, UAP, Seita, Usinor/Sacilor, Péchiney, and a majority stake in Renault (with the state keeping a 44 percent share).

More remarkable than the Right's privatizations, however, has been the acceleration of this program under the Socialist-Communist-Green coalition that took office in June 1997. Prime Minister Jospin prefers to talk about "private sector participation," but the effect—returning state-owned companies to the private sector—is the same. Under Jospin and his first finance minister, Dominique Strauss-Kahn, the state privatized companies previously thought of as untouchable, such as Thomson-CSF, Aérospatiale, Crédit Lyonnais, CIC, GAN, and AGF. The Socialists maintained majority ownership of big, highly symbolic companies like France Télécom and Air France—but the fact that Air France was even partially privatized, and under Communist transport minister Jean-Claude Gayssot, shows how far the country had come since the 1972 Common Program of the Left called for the nationalization of practically all French industry. Between 1997 and 2000 Jospin partially privatized France Télécom in several stages, bringing the state's share down to 54 percent.

By the start of 2001, the Jospin government had already sold off more than 240 billion francs in state enterprises, more than the six previous French governments—including the "neoliberal" Chirac government of 1986–88—put together.[20] Privatization also seems to be gaining acceptance from French public opinion, even on the Left. As recently as 1995, 52 percent of voters on the French Left had a "positive attitude" toward nationalization and only 32 percent had a positive attitude toward privatization; by 1999 the former had fallen to 39 percent and the latter had grown to 44 percent.[21] As Le Monde said of Jospin in December 2000, "He privatized more than any other government ever had; but never had the sales of public companies generated so little controversy."[22]

There are, of course, limits to how far privatization will go in France. Public utilities, such as railways and electricity, for example, are still state owned and there seems to be little interest in privatizing them (unlike in the United States and Britain). Key segments of the French political spectrum, including the Communists and significant parts of the Socialist Party, oppose any further privatization.[23] Still, it is striking that the French state, which in 1982 had almost total control of the financial and insurance sectors, is now almost completely out of both. And the European Commission is even requiring the utilities to deregulate and open themselves up to competition. As one senior French executive puts it, "The time when Bercy [the French Ministry of the Economy] lorded over the corporate world is past. Today, the monopolies are regulated by independent authorities, and the private sector by the market. Except for a few key issues, the state no longer has a say."[24]

The Stock Market

Partly due to privatization, and partly due to the growing need to raise capital in a global market, the 1990s saw the marked development of the French stock market—in terms both of increasing participation among the French and of increased openness to foreign investment in French companies. The total capitalization of the French stock market has risen from around 33 percent of GDP in the mid-1980s to nearly 100 percent.[25] Just as in the "Anglo-Saxon" economies of which France has traditionally been so critical, this move away from bank debt and family finance to more volatile stocks has forced companies to focus on shareholder value and to closely follow the dictates of the global market—lest ever-more-mobile global capital flow abroad.[26] Vivendi chairman Jean-Marie Messier has made it clear that French companies cannot "refuse to be listed on the stock market when most acquisitions are now made through the exchange of stocks."[27]

The initial modernization of the French financial sector, long a key component of the *dirigiste* system, occurred under the government of Laurent Fabius, with Pierre Bérégovoy as finance minister.[28] The government instituted a money market in which large companies could raise funds, thus bypassing the near-exclusiveness of state-controlled banks, and made it accessible to all sorts of investors—banks, households, and companies. New saving instruments were created, such as certificates of deposit, capital bills, and negotiable Treasury bonds. The Marché à Terme des Instruments Financiers (MATIF), the French financial futures market, opened in 1986. These reforms, undertaken by a Socialist government, fundamentally transformed the structure of the French financial sector and paved the way for the liberalization of credit, which would, in turn, improve the competitiveness of the French economy.

The greatest boost to popular participation in the stock market from within France came with Chirac's wave of privatization in 1986–88, which increased the number of French shareholders to 6.5 million, compared with an average of just 1.5 million for 1978–82.[29] After the 1987 crash, market participation fell to around 5 million and stayed at approximately that level during the depressed market of the early 1990s. In 2000, however, it began to rise again, with 400,000 new shareholders raising the total to 5.6 million. At around 10 percent of the adult population, this lags behind market participation in the United States (22 percent) or Britain (15 percent), but it is high by historical standards in France. When owners of mutual funds and corporate bonds are included, the total rises to 9 million, or one out of every five adults.[30] Moreover, stock market participation among younger investors is booming. In 1999 participation rose by 27 percent for those under twenty-five years old, and by 15 percent for twenty-five to thirty-four year olds, suggesting that the generational trend is toward greater reliance on stocks.

More important, perhaps, and more directly the result of globalization, is the growing foreign participation in French markets. Whereas as recently as 1985 foreign ownership of French firms was only around 10 percent, it is estimated that more than 40 percent of French shares are now held by foreigners—mostly large U.S. and British pension funds.[31] In this sense France is far more "globalized" than the United States (where about 7 percent of shares are held by foreigners), Japan (around 10 percent), Germany (around 10 percent), or even the United Kingdom (under 16 percent).[32] As table 2-1 shows, the majority of shares of key French companies like Société Générale, Alcatel, Danone, and Suez are held abroad.

Another sign of the impact of globalization and new technology on French stock markets is the Nouveau Marché, the equivalent of the NASDAQ in the United States, focused on the stocks of young technology companies. Created in 1996, the Nouveau Marché grew from eighty-one companies in 1999 to 113 in 2000, and its index rose by 135 percent during that period, reaching a market capitalization of $14 billion by the end of 1999, compared with $4 billion just one year earlier.[33] During 2001, the Nouveau Marché suffered significant losses along with its counterparts in the United States and elsewhere, but the existence and growth of such a market showed France's readiness to participate in the high risk but high stakes business of the new economy.

Finally, France's conversion to the new economy in the financial sphere is evidenced in the development of stock options, traditionally seen as an example of Anglo-Saxon-style jungle capitalism run amok. With some 34,500 people in the forty biggest quoted companies participating in such schemes (1 percent of all employees in these companies), France now has the highest level of stock option distribution among European countries, second worldwide only to the United States.[34]

To be sure, the reliance on stock options remains controversial in France. Critics blame it for growing income inequality, as corporate executives reap large rewards even while the unemployment rate remains high. Indeed, in late 1999—partly inspired by the $24 million in stock options reportedly awarded departing Elf chief executive officer Philippe Jaffré when the company was taken over by TotalFina—Socialist and Commu-

Table 2-1. *Nonresident Shareholders of Key French Companies*

Company	Sector	Nonresident shareholders (percent)	North American and British shareholders (percent)	Market capitalization (billions of euros)
Dexia	Finance	74.3	11.2	17,490
AGF[a]	Finance	73.4	7.9	12,118
TotalFina Elf[b]	Energy	65.0	20.0	129,656
Cap Gemini	Information services	64.0	31.0	15,507
Vivendi Universal	Media services	61.6	24.6	80,469
Alsom	Equipment	61.5	47.0	7,215
Aventis	Pharmaceuticals	58.0	31.6	69,236
Axa	Finance	52.0	28.0	56,040
EADS[c]	Aerospace	50.9	5.5	19,291
Alcatel	Electronics	50.0	40.0	33,942
Lafarge	Construction	49.8	29.0	13,818
Michelin[b]	Automobile equipment	48.0	24.0	5,231
Lagardère	Holding	47.5	27.0	8,296
Danone	Food	47.0	26.0	22,693
Accor	Hotel	40.8	16.9	n.a.
BNP Paribas	Finance	40.0	n.a.	n.a.
Saint-Gobain	Construction	40.0	22.0	14,173
Crédit Lyonnais	Finance	35.0	5.0	14,582
Valeo	Automobile equipment	35.0	19.0	40,063
Schneider Electric	Electrical equipment	34.0	22.0	10,235
Carrefour	Distribution	30.5	12.0	44,731
Pinault Printemps	Distribution	30.5	n.a.	23,516
Air Liquide	Raw materials	29.3	15.5	14,887
Sanofi-Synthelabo	Pharmaceuticals	27.2	18.1	51,175
Bouygues	Construction	25.0	17.0	14,054
Dassault Systèmes	Software	21.1	14.0	6,025
L'Oréal	Cosmetics	20.0	6.5	50,411
Sodexho Alliance	Hospitality	19.1	10.5	7,979
Renault	Automobile	19.0	14.0	11,977
LVMH	Luxury goods	17.8	8.1	31,966
Thales (ex-Thomson CSF)	Electronic equipment	13.9	11.0	7,873
France Télécom	Telecommunications	10.0	4.0	68,075
Orange	Telecommunications	10.0	4.0	48,675
Casino Guichard	Distribution	9.4	5.7	10,920

n.a. = not available.

Source: "Les poids croissant des actionnaires anglo-saxons," *Le Monde*, June 15, 2000, p. 22. Data on foreign capital investment are from a study commissioned by *Le Monde* from the U.S. firm Georgeson Shareholder and include the CAC 40. Market capitalization data are from Bloomberg.

a. Includes Allianz (53.9 percent).

b. Second column does not include British shareholders.

c. Includes Daimler (30.3 percent) and Casa (5.5 percent).

nist members of parliament introduced a bill calling for the tax rate on capital gains from stock options to be raised from 40 percent to up to 54 percent, the highest income tax rate in France.[35] The government—led by Finance Minister Laurent Fabius and pushed by French industry—opposed the tax rise on the grounds that stock options increase business incentives, foster entrepreneurship, and stimulate business (not concepts traditionally associated with French Socialist governments). Ultimately, in April 2000 a complex compromise was reached between the Socialist government and its socialist critics, leaving the lower tax rate in place as long as the options were held for at least six years and also applying lower tax rates for capital gains of less than 1 million francs.[36]

Because global investors seek to maximize returns on their investments and have a multitude of options around the world, the use of stock options will be a major test of France's adaptation to globalization. So far, it seems to be successful.

Industry

Globalization is changing French corporate culture dramatically, and French companies are thriving as a result. This is apparent not only in the booming export trade and the annual trade surpluses since 1992, but also in the growing levels of overseas investment by French firms, which, as shown in figure 2-2, has risen sharply over the past several years to some $170 billion in 2000. The globalization of French industry is also evident in the unprecedented wave of mergers and acquisitions that French firms have used either to acquire foreign firms or to prepare to compete with them. French companies are now among the most respected global players, and are headed by a new breed of young and aggressive corporate leaders.[37] As table 2-2 shows, many well-known French companies derive the major portion of their annual turnovers from international sales, including Michelin (85 percent), Alcatel (83 percent), Dassault (82 percent), Louis Vuitton Moët Hennessy (81 percent), Axa (75 percent), and Publicis (75 percent).[38] As Messier says, it is now "impossible, in telecommunications and most other major lines of business, to be only a national actor. You have to be at least European and if possible global."[39]

Although mergers and acquisitions (particularly hostile ones) were once seen in France as among the worst excesses of Anglo-Saxon jungle capitalism, they have risen in value from an average of around $15 billion per year in 1990–95 to more than $50 billion per year in 1997 and 1998 and over $70 billion in 1999.[40] The past several years have seen a wave of global acquisitions by French companies. In spring 2001, for example, Vivendi—once exclusively a water services company—announced that it was purchasing the online music business MP3.com and the educational publisher Houghton Mifflin, while Alcatel opened multibillion-dollar

Figure 2-2. *French Foreign Direct Investment, Inflows and Outflows,*
1995–2000

Billions of dollars

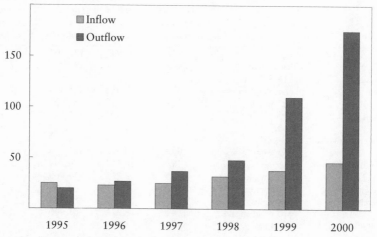

Source: French Ministry of Finance (www.finances.gouv.fr).

merger talks with Lucent, a U.S.-based producer of telecommunication
equipment.[41] Less than a year before, in June 2000, Vivendi completed the
$34 billion purchase of Seagram's (owner of Hollywood's Universal Stu-
dios and Polygram Records) on the same day as Publicis purchased the
noted British advertising firm Saatchi and Saatchi for $4 billion. These
acquisitions came less than two months after France Télécom had enhanced its international presence by acquiring the British mobile phone
company Orange, and just four months after the French computing con-
sultant Cap Gemini announced its $11 billion takeover of the U.S.-based
accounting firm Ernst & Young.

The previous year was equally active. During 1999, the French car maker
Renault, after decades of government support and bailouts and a painful
restructuring in the early 1990s, acquired a 36.8 percent stake in the Japanese giant Nissan. The two French luxury goods groups Pinault Printemps
La Redoute (PPR) and Louis Vuitton Moët Hennessy (LVMH) battled for
control of Gucci. TotalFina purchased Elf to create the world's fourth-
largest oil company. Banque Nationale de Paris (BNP) completed a hostile
takeover of Paribas. And retailer Carrefour both took over Promodès, creating the world's second-largest retailer, and teamed up with Oracle and
Sears to create a global Internet supply exchange.[42] Carrefour has a pres-

Table 2-2.   *Profile of Key French Companies and Revenues Derived Abroad, 1999*

Name	Industry	Turnover (billions of francs)	Net profit (millions of francs)	Number of employees	Percent of revenues derived abroad
TotalFina Elf	Oil	492.0	21,969	127,000	73.0
Carrefour	Distribution	340.5	5,891	297,300	38.0
Vivendi	Services/ communication	272.9	8,387	275,000	42.8
PSA	Automobile	248.0	4,782	166,000	64.6
Renault	Automobile	246.7	3,503	160,000	63.4
EDF	Electricity	209.9	4,690	132,500	18.6
Suez-Lyonnaise	Services/ communication	206.6	9,512	222,000	66.6
France Télécom	Telecommunications	178.4	17,712	174,300	12.8
Alcatel	Telecom equipment	150.9	4,225	115,700	85.0
Saint-Gobain	Construction	150.2	7,872	164,700	65.3
Aventis	Chemicals/ pharmaceuticals	134.2	−8,922	101,000	51.0
PPR	Distribution	124.0	4,067	89,200	48.1
Casino	Distribution	122.0	1,706	85,000	18.8
SNCF	Railroads	106.8	336	210,900	20.2
Alstom	Railroad equipment	106.4	2,289	120,700	79.8
Bouygues	BTP/communication	103.6	407	111,300	36.5
La Poste	Mail	100.5	1,860	291,700	. . .
Michelin	Tires	90.5	1,010	130,400	86.0
Usinor	Iron and steel	89.2	−1,168	64,100	67.2
Danone	Food	87.2	4,474	76,000	62.7
Aerospatiale Matra	Aerospace/defense	84.6	200	52,400	72.5
Lagardère	Defense/ communication	80.7	1,581	49,300	63.7
L'Oréal	Cosmetics	70.5	5,425	42,200	83.1
Lafarge	Construction	68.9	4,028	70,900	78.5
Air France	Air transport	67.7	2,322	53,800	53.0
Pechiney	Aluminum, packaging	62.3	1,706	29,840	59.8
Gaz de France	Gas distribution	59.7	2,747	31,200	5.8
Eridania	Farm/produce	59.0	59	23,000	78.9
LVMH	Luxury goods	55.8	4,546	38,300	80.0
Schneider Electric	Electric equipment	54.4	3,155	67,500	82.0

Source: Le Monde, *Bilan du Monde 2001*, p. 185.

ence in twenty-six countries and has become the largest retailer in some of these, for example, Argentina, where it performs better than Wal-Mart.[43]

Not only are French companies making acquisitions abroad, but France is also becoming more open to investment from abroad, overcoming its previous aversion to foreign control in key sectors, like banking. Foreign direct investment (FDI) in France reached a record level of nearly $50 billion in 2000 (see figure 2-2); in terms of volume, France was the third largest recipient of FDI in the world—and the second in Europe, after the United Kingdom.

Another example of France's growing openness to foreign direct investment can be found in the April 2000 takeover of Crédit Commercial de France (CCF) by the U.K. bank HSBC. Founded in 1894 and headquartered on the Champs Elysées, the CCF became the first French bank to fall into foreign hands, something French governments had long sought to prevent. Only the previous year, the Jospin government had made clear that it did not want to see a foreign bidder win control of Crédit Lyonnais or play a role in the takeover battle going on among BNP, Société Générale, and Paribas. Now, however, the French government stood aside and allowed the unprecedented takeover to go forward. The chairman of CCF, Charles de Croisset, said he did not see "where the taboo is," and noted that around 75 percent of the bank's shareholders were already foreigners.[44]

Although French companies have undergone a radical change, remnants of *dirigisme* remain. Some skeptics of France's recent transformation, for example, point out that in 1999 the Banque de France tried to intervene in the BNP–Société Générale–Paribas takeover battle. This move by BNP provided an opportunity for France to create a banking heavyweight (an old-style "national champion") if the three banks united their forces, as the Banque de France wished. What is significant in this episode, however, is not that the state tried to intervene, but that in the end it failed to produce the outcome it wanted. BNP succeeded in acquiring Paribas, but not Société Générale—and therefore a French banking champion was not born.[45]

Similarly, many observers have used the aborted takeover attempt of Orangina to argue that France is not really changing. In September 1999, the minister of the economy blocked the 5 billion franc sale of the soft drink Orangina by Pernod-Ricard to Coca-Cola. This move was interpreted as a classic example of France standing up to the "American challenge"—how could the French let their only internationally recognized soft drink be taken over by the company once seen as the symbol of American cultural and economic imperialism? In fact, the real (and ironic) rationale for the intervention was on Anglo-Saxon-style competition grounds, for Coca-Cola and Orangina together would have represented 77 percent of soft drinks sold outside the home market.[46] The fact that the whole episode will most likely end with Pepsi taking over Orangina suggests that the French state is indeed stepping back from intervention. The successful takeover of Elf by TotalFina provides another good example. According to TotalFina chief executive officer Thierry Desmarest, "The lesson is that France is changing rapidly. We have shown in this merger that companies can make an amicable deal without the government. Ten years ago . . . the government would have decided the outcome of this."[47]

Economic Openness

Despite its protectionist tradition and reputation, France has responded to globalization not by putting up new barriers to trade but, for the most part, by bringing them down. To be sure, there has been an underlying current of mercantilism in French economic policy throughout the postwar period, as illustrated by the trade-distorting industrial policies of the 1960s, 1970s, and early 1980s. And even as tariffs fell within Europe as a result of the creation and development of the European Union, nontariff barriers to trade and voluntary restraint agreements, particularly with non-EU countries, rose. France's infamous arrangement in 1982 for all video-cassette recorders imported from Japan to pass through a single customs clearinghouse in Poitiers is a prime example.[48] Still, Mitterrand's decision in 1983 not to raise tariffs and quotas, even in the face of mounting trade deficits, was an important sign of recognition that France could not shut itself off from international competition.

In the mid-1990s, with unemployment seemingly on an ever-upward path and emerging markets apparently threatening French jobs even more by offering low-cost labor, France was faced again with the dilemma of what would soon be called globalization. As the final phase of the Uruguay Round of the General Agreement on Tariffs and Trade got under way, politicians and much of French public opinion alleged a clear link between rising unemployment and globalization as manifested by international economic openness. The debate over the validity of protectionism was framed in large part by the Arthuis Report, a 1993 study by the French Senate that claimed that the French economy was threatened by *délocalisation*—the loss of jobs to low-wage countries.[49] Largely ignoring other potential causes of unemployment in France—such as labor market rigidities and the overvalued franc—the Arthuis Report suggested that some 3 million to 5 million French jobs were threatened by the prospect of the transfer of production facilities to low-wage countries.[50]

Notwithstanding the public debate, however, the French response to this alleged threat remained largely rhetorical. Economists (even French ones) and the rare politician, such as Patrick Devedjian of the center Right Rassemblement pour la République (RPR), pointed out that the extent of French trade with and investment in poor countries was too small to account for anywhere near the number of jobs that were supposed to have been lost to these factors, and in any case, France has a trade surplus outside the EU.[51] The government resisted calls to introduce new trade barriers, with Prime Minister Edouard Balladur arguing that "the French economy, like the European economy, is too open to the world to sustain the closing of its markets."[52]

As the 1990s progressed, the issue of protectionism faded further, particularly as unemployment started to fall in 1998 and France continued to run trade surpluses—in every year since 1994. Although important sectors like agriculture remain sheltered from global competition and several high-profile trade disputes, such as those on bananas, Airbus, and airplane hush kits, continue to attract headlines and create transatlantic resentment, the French economy today is more open than it has ever been. As shown in figure 2-3, French trade (exports plus imports) as a share of GDP, at only 24.9 percent in 1962, has been rising for the past thirty years: from 32.4 percent in 1972 to 45.5 percent in 1982 to 44 percent in 1992 and up to 49 percent in 1997.[53] France now enjoys the same level of trade openness as Germany (49 percent), slightly less than the United Kingdom (57 percent), but nearly twice as much as the United States (25 percent) or Japan (21 percent). Economist Patrick Messerlin, referring to the EU's role in bringing down French trade barriers, rightly calls this gradual conversion liberalization "by proxy," but it has been liberalization nonetheless.[54]

Monetary and Exchange Rate Policy

Monetary and exchange rate policy is another area that has been greatly affected by and has adapted remarkably to globalization. When international trade played a much less significant role than today in French economic policy, monetary policy was seen primarily as a domestic tool—it was frequently manipulated in an attempt to stimulate growth and jobs, with little regard for the implications for the level of the franc, which depreciated throughout the 1950s, 1960s, and 1970s. As the French economy became more open, however—primarily within the European Common Market but also vis-à-vis the rest of the world—the consequences

Figure 2-3.   *Trade as a Share of French GDP, 1950–99*

Percent of GDP

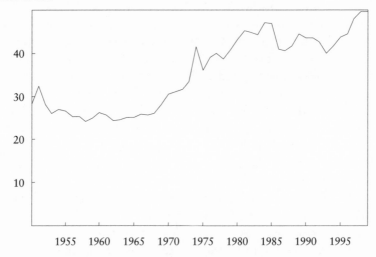

Source: Penn World Tables and World Bank, *World Development Indicators, 2001* (CD-ROM).

of a declining exchange rate could no longer be ignored. Without corresponding cuts in the government's deficit spending, the devaluations only stimulated inflation, quickly leading, in a vicious cycle, to the need for a further depreciation.

After the turbulent decade of the 1970s, when the French economy was buffeted first by wildly fluctuating oil prices (with the Organization of Petroleum Exporting Countries' price increases of 1974 and 1979), high inflation, and an unstable exchange rate, President Giscard d'Estaing sought to use the European Monetary System to shield the franc from exchange rate variations, at least in relation to its most important trading partners. Mitterrand's economic experiment of 1981 severely strained this system, leading to devaluations of the franc within the EMS in October 1981, June 1982, and March 1983, the result of which was finally to convince the French that they had no choice but to pursue a stable level for the franc in an increasingly integrated world economy. As noted above, Mitterrand's austerity plan, initiated in 1984, succeeded in curbing French inflation rates, and after small corrections in the level of the franc in 1986 and 1987 (and a temporary widening of the bands of the European exchange rate mechanism in 1993, following German unification) the franc was not devalued within the EMS again.[55] By the late 1980s, French inflation rates were actually lower than those of traditionally inflation-conscious Germany, even if French interest rates remained higher than Germany's because of the French reputation for profligacy, which would take a few more years to overcome.

This *franc fort* (strong franc) policy—bolstered by the independence of the Banque de France in 1993, a dramatic sign of France's new thinking about economic management—has remained in place to this day, and shows no sign of changing. It was a key element in making possible the adoption of the European single currency, the euro, in 1999, capping a long struggle by French leaders to implement a more "Germanic" monetary model. While the single currency clearly has not removed all potential concerns about exchange rates and globalization—as the European debate about the euro's exchange rate vis-à-vis the dollar shows—it has once and for all stabilized the franc in relation to eleven of France's largest trading partners—who account for half of French exports and imports.[56]

Indeed, the debate on the euro-dollar exchange rate provides a telling comment on the degree to which French economic policy and thinking have changed. In February 2000, while Hans Eichel, the German finance minister, argued that the weak euro was not so bad after all, the governor of the French central bank, Jean-Claude Trichet, made the case for a stronger currency.[57] Again, in September 2000, after the euro had fallen to its lowest level ever against the dollar ($0.87), German chancellor Gerhard Schroeder was more complacent than the French, saying that the exchange rate was "more of a reason to be happy than concerned" because it helped to stimulate European growth.[58] As Tony Barber of the *Financial Times* put it, "France, a country once identified with inflation, devaluation and other disagreeable monetary habits, is starting to displace Germany as Europe's champion of a strong currency and as an engine of economic growth."[59]

Taxation

Perhaps the most powerful example of the predominant role of the state in French capitalism has been taxation, the share of the country's overall production taken by the state. As noted above, the French state spends more than half (54 percent) of the country's GDP, and France's overall tax burden—nearly 46 percent, including social charges—is among the highest in the world; among Eurozone countries, only Finland, Luxembourg, and Belgium take a greater percentage of GDP.[60]

Yet here, too, French attitudes and policies are changing rapidly. Tax rates began to fall in 1999 and early 2000, when the Socialists passed two separate laws that reduced the tax burden by 80 billion francs. The cuts affected personal income tax, value added tax (VAT), and property tax, leading to a reduction in the real tax burden by as much as 1 percent of GDP.[61] In the April 2000 rate cut, VAT was reduced from 20.6 percent to 19.6 percent, at a cost to the Treasury of 18 billion francs (or 2.74 million euros).[62] These cuts were followed in August–September 2000 with the announcement of what Finance Minister Laurent Fabius called the largest tax cutting and tax reform plan the country had seen for more than fifty years.[63] Presenting his plan, Fabius described France's tax burden as a "major structural handicap" to the French economy, "because of its size and the way it is shared." He promised "lasting control of public and defense spending, and ambitious reform of the whole state apparatus," focusing the state on its "essential functions."[64] This is remarkable language from a French Socialist and testifies to the degree to which French thinking on taxation is changing, or being forced to change, in a globalized world economy.

Specifically, the new tax plan calls for an additional 120 billion francs in tax cuts for the period 2001–03, which, added to the 80 billion francs in cuts announced earlier, means a total tax reduction of 200 billion francs for 2000–03. The new plan includes a 70 billion franc reduction in indirect taxes (mainly VAT); a 45 billion franc reduction in income tax; the elimination of the automobile tax, costing 13 billion francs; and a 20 billion to 30 billion franc reduction of the Contribution Sociale Généralisée (CSG), a broad-based levy for social spending.[65] Strikingly, the plan also includes the elimination of the 10 percent surcharge on businesses (*l'impôt sur les sociétés*) that had been instituted by RPR prime minister Alain Juppé, and a reduction in the top rate of income tax from 54 percent to 52.5 percent in 2003. While this seems a small reduction, and it is true that the cuts are proportionally greater for lower income levels (as would be expected from a left-wing government), the very idea of a Socialist-led government reducing the top level of tax is, as Le Monde said, no less than a "great conversion."[66] It was the Socialists, after all, who in 1983 raised the top income tax rate from 60 percent to 65 percent, and who had seen it reduced by the Right twice, to 56.8 percent in 1988 and to 54 percent in 1996.[67] Assuming the overall economy grows at projected levels for the next three years, Fabius's plans would bring France's overall tax burden (taxes plus social charges) down from its historic peak of 45.7 percent in 1999 to the 1995 level of 43.7 percent in 2003.[68]

To be sure, much of France's new tax-cutting fervor is simply due to renewed economic growth, and the proposed tax cuts are somewhat less ambitious than those passed in other European countries, including Germany.[69] French tax rates will remain comparatively high within the Organization for Economic Cooperation and Development (OECD), even if the Fabius plan is implemented. Moreover, not all of the Left is enthusiastic about the plan—if the economy slows, one can be sure that the Communists, the Greens, and the Left wing of the Socialist Party will want to slow tax cuts before they agree to cuts in spending.[70] Public opinion is also skeptical of tax cuts, at least for the relatively well-off; according to a poll in May 2000, 57 percent supported increasing taxes on capital gains (with 36 percent opposed), 45 percent were for higher taxes on stock options (with 34 percent opposed), and only 34 percent supported tax cuts for upper income brackets (with 63 percent opposed).[71]

Nonetheless, it is clear that the government's tax plans have been motivated in large part by the need to compete both within the EU and in a globalized world, where differences in taxation rates—whether on corporations, income, capital gains, or wealth or social charges—can lead individuals, companies, and especially entrepreneurs to base themselves abroad. Indeed, tax flight has been a significant problem in France. It received particular prominence in early 2000, when Laetitia Casta, the model chosen to symbolize Marianne (the female symbol of the French republic), was reported to have moved to London in order to pay less tax.[72] Although Casta later denied having changed her official place of residence for tax purposes, the question of whether high marginal tax rates were making France less competitive had been raised. The tax cuts decided in 1999–2000 have been designed in part to answer it.

Labor Regulations

The most evident exception to France's economic adaptation to globalization would seem—on the surface, at least—to be in the area of labor regulation. Not only have France's efforts to make its employment policies more flexible been extremely modest since the early 1990s, but the flagship of the Jospin government's economic legislation has apparently been an effort to regulate the workplace further—through the *Réduction du temps de travail* (RTT). The proposal to reduce the number of hours worked in a week from thirty-nine to thirty-five, without a corresponding reduction in wages, was a key element of the Socialists' electoral platform in 1997 and arguably helped them to win the election. Proponents of the plan, led by then labor minister Martine Aubry, claimed that the new approach would create a million jobs and help lower the French unemployment rate of 12 percent at the time.[73] Through two laws passed in 1998 and 1999, the statutory work week was set at thirty-five hours as of January 1, 2000, for firms with more than twenty employees, and as of January 1, 2002, for smaller firms, with overtime payments required for those who worked more than thirty-five hours. Most state employees, not covered by these laws, have negotiated thirty-five-hour work weeks for themselves. By May 2001, more than 73,000 firms, employing 6.8 million workers, had signed agreements for a thirty-five-hour work week.[74]

The main goals of the RTT, according to the government, were job creation, competitiveness, improved working conditions, and a better balance between career and personal life.[75] The measure appears to reflect the *dirigiste* belief that the state is better suited than the market to allocate labor resources. In an integrating world economy in which other countries—not just in Western Europe or North America, but in Asia as well—are relaxing labor regulations and letting workers work many more hours, the idea of limiting work time without a corresponding reduction in pay would seem to be a prohibitive tax on business, incompatible with the supposed requirements of globalization. It has certainly been criticized as such by the "Anglo-Saxon" press and the French Right, and most severely by the French employers' association, the Mouvement des Entreprises de France (MEDEF).[76]

Yet the implementation of the RTT shows how France is taking globalization into account even as it seeks to maintain traditional social protections and to appease the political Left. Instead of being a major burden on employers, the thirty-five-hour work week has in fact increased their flexibility and in some ways has decreased their costs. In exchange for the shorter work week, employers were allowed to negotiate new deals on flexible work time, and often to demand wage restraint as part of the new labor contracts. Because the law requires only an *average* of thirty-five hours per week over the entire year, firms have also been able to be responsive to demand cycles, thus reducing their overtime costs. For example, Samsonite's employees have agreed to work forty-two hours per week in the summer, when demand for their products is high, and only thirty-two hours per week in the winter. Similarly, at retailer Carrefour, cashiers have agreed to adjust their duties and schedules according to the volume of customers in a store.[77] This unexpected—or at least little emphasized—aspect of the thirty-five-hour work week has helped French companies implement the legislation in a way that has avoided the widespread reduction in competitiveness feared at the start.

Given the very great variety of factors that affect employment figures, it is impossible to say for sure whether the increased employment claimed by the government—some 265,000 jobs created or preserved by the RTT as of June 2001—is the result of the program, but it is just as hard to argue that the legislation has been a great economic burden.[78] In 1999, for example, 374,800 new jobs were created, a 2.5 percent increase from 1998 and the most jobs created in France in a single year since the 1970s.[79] In 2000, more than 500,000 jobs were created, the most ever in a single year, and by mid-2001 unemployment had fallen to 8.7 percent.[80] Indeed, by provoking new and more flexible labor arrangements, and by giving the Jospin government political cover for some of its more liberal policies, the RTT is proving to be the opposite of the economic burden claimed by its initial critics.[81]

Computers and the Internet

Just a few years ago, France's apparent inability or unwillingness to join the information technology revolution—mainly in the form of personal computers and the Internet—was widely seen as proof that the country was incapable of adapting to globalization and the requirements of the new economy. Statistics on computer and Internet use seemed to confirm this judgment. As of 1998, for example, only 16 percent of French households had a personal computer, well behind the 20 to 25 percent in the United Kingdom and Germany and 40 percent in the United States.[82] France was even further behind in Internet use: only 500,000 French households or businesses had Internet connections, compared with 4 million in the United Kingdom and 40 million in the United States.[83] According to the *Computer Industry Almanac,* at the end of 1998 just 0.8 percent of the French population regularly used the Internet, compared with 1.5 percent in Germany, 2.2 percent in the United Kingdom, 3.5 percent in Sweden, and 8.7 percent in the United States (France had 2.79 million regular users, compared with 7.14 million in Germany, 8.10 million in Great Britain, and 76.5 million in the United States).[84]

There were several plausible explanations for why France lagged behind other advanced industrialized countries in the Internet revolution: relatively high Internet access costs; less fluency with, or an aversion to using, English, the language of nearly 80 percent of web pages; a tradition of relying on a centralized state for information; or the existence of the Minitel, France's own telephone-line-based information service, which is still used in 6.5 million French homes and accounts for 85 million hours of connection time annually.[85] Indeed, in his 1999 bestseller on globalization, *The Lexus and the Olive Tree*, Thomas L. Friedman titled one chapter "Buy Taiwan, Hold Italy, Sell France," advice based largely on the assumption that France was not adapting its information technology to globalization.[86] France, however, has been catching up.[87] According to the French Association of Internet Service Providers, in January 1998 only 540,000 French residents were connected to the Internet, for a collective total usage that month of 4 million hours. By January 2000, the number of connections had risen to more than 3 million, for a collective total usage of 25.3 million hours.[88] This was a more than fivefold increase in numbers of users and sixfold increase in connection time in a period of just two years. By April 2001, the number of Internet connections had risen to 6 million, a gain of 50 percent over the previous year.[89] French PC use has also been rising, to 27 percent of households in 2000, compared with just 15 percent in 1996 and 16 percent in 1998.[90] As the next chapter shows, the French are indeed concerned about domination of American ideas and English language via the Internet and have taken some measures to address these concerns.[91] But they no longer seem to be keeping the French from plugging in to the wired world.

Public opinion data also show a rise in French levels of comfort with the Internet, even as they show how much ground must still be traveled. For example, according to a February 2000 poll, as recently as May 1996 no less than 95 percent of those surveyed said they had never tried using the Internet (5 percent said that they had done so). By February 2000, however, some 32 percent of those surveyed said they "had tried" or were "regular users" of the Internet.[92] Clearly, with 68 percent of its citizens never having tried the Internet, France still has a long way to go in its embrace of modern communications technology and it still lags behind many of its European partners and well behind the United States. But the trend is in the right direction.

Conclusion

These dramatic changes in how the French economy is run have not occurred suddenly, even though their cumulated results are only now beginning to affect popular perceptions. The move away from *dirigisme* and

toward economic liberalism has been driven overwhelmingly by globalization—first in the form of Europeanization and the single market in the
1980s, then in a broader sense in the 1990s. Globalization has forced
French politicians, on the Right as on the Left, to adopt a new paradigm
for the role of the state, which we explore in chapter 4. This phenomenon
is not unique to France: the "New Democrats" in the United States and
the "New Labour" in the United Kingdom have (from different starting
points) gone even further than the French in their conversion to economic
liberalism, proposing tax cuts and welfare reforms that would once have
been unthinkable for left-of-center parties. What marks France relative to
these other countries, however, is the distance policymakers have had to
travel—both intellectually and in terms of actual policy changes—given
the traditional role of the state in the economy.

To be sure, while France has undergone a dramatic adaptation of its
economic structure in order to conform to the requirements of competition in a globalizing world, this adaptation has not been without problems and opposition. Change is slow, and old habits die hard. For instance,
when fuel prices rose considerably in September 2000, several sectoral
interests (such as truckers) resorted to the old reflex of blaming the government and asking the state to intervene to lower prices (by lowering fuel
taxes).[93] And the fact that the French state gave in to the protesters and
made concessions—unlike other European governments in the same situation—serves as a reminder that France has not completely bought into
the new free market paradigm.[94] Even more striking was the general out-
rage provoked in France in April 2001 when British retailer Marks &
Spencer decided to close all its French outlets and the French food group
Danone announced it was laying off over 1,800 workers, despite the fact
that the company remained profitable. These examples suggest that it is
still not easy for the French to accept the full consequences of an integrated world economy operating on free market principles.[95] The political
reaction to Danone's layoffs—including a boycott of the company, advocated by numerous labor unions and politicians, and legislation proposed
by the Socialist-led government to constrain the ability of profitable companies to release workers—were clear signs that for all the changes in
French economic thinking, a reversal of the free market trend remains a
possibility.[96]

Moreover, despite all the progress discussed in this chapter, several
areas of the economy are still in need of reform if France is to compete
globally. One of the most important tasks is to enhance the climate for

entrepreneurship. According to the OECD, because of extensive legal and administrative formalities, it takes about fifteen weeks to start a company in France, significantly longer than in other OECD countries. In France, even after a new company is registered, its founders must overcome up to twenty-one administrative hurdles (depending on the type of company), compared with a maximum of thirteen in Japan, eight in Germany, four in the United Kingdom, and just two in the United States.[97] Among OECD countries, only Italy has a higher number of such barriers to entrepreneurship than France, and none have more administrative regulations. The government is making modest efforts to facilitate business creation, and polls show that more and more French people are attracted by the idea of starting a business; but until it becomes easier to do so, France risks losing entrepreneurs to other countries in a globalized world.[98]

Another great challenge for the years to come is to reform the state itself, including the pension system and the civil service (encompassing the tax administration and national education). Yet each time a French government attempt such reform, it seems that the country is not yet ready. In winter 1995, for example, the Juppé government attempted to cut a bloated state sector in which it estimated there were about 500,000 jobs too many, but strikes forced the government to back down and discredited the prime minister.[99] Four years later, in spring 1999, the Jospin government similarly tried to reform the education and finance ministries. In the latter case, the reform was an apparently sensible one that would have merged the tax assessment and collection functions into a single, "one-stop" system, making life easier for taxpayers and reducing the finance ministry's personnel budget, which accounted for no less than 81 percent of the total. Again, however, state unions and workers mobilized, shut down Paris with strikes, and forced the government to retreat.[100] Opinion polls showed that in both cases the French public overwhelmingly supported the strikers.[101] If one can judge by the unsuccessful experiences of successive governments, Right and Left, in tackling these issues, the reform of the state—on which such a large share of the French working population still depends for employment—will be one of the greatest economic challenges of all. The limits to France's adaptation to a liberal world market economy have expanded greatly over the years, but they are now being tested.

CHAPTER THREE

Trade, Culture, and Identity

"France wants to be the motor of cultural diversity in the world."

Lionel Jospin, July 21, 2000

"Vive le roquefort libre!"

Alain Rollat, Le Monde, *September 9, 1999*

If the impact of globalization on France were merely economic, the French would probably not find it so problematic. As the preceding chapter made clear, the French economy is adapting remarkably well to the requirements of globalization; for many, the loss of state control and growing inequalities that result from globalization may be a price worth paying for increased prosperity and jobs. The real threat from globalization is thus not economic but cultural: it is not so much the disappearance of *dirigisme* that worries the French, but the disappearance of France itself. Like others in Europe and elsewhere around the world, but even more so, the French are concerned that globalization, and the accompanying harmonization of culture, threatens their distinctive identity and many of the values, customs, and traditions of which they are so proud.

The desire to maintain a culture with wide appeal and a concomitant fear of cultural domination are hardly new issues in France. Throughout the postwar period, France has periodically undergone "identity crises"—

often, but not always, focused on concern about the cultural domination of the United States. What is new today is the way in which French identity and culture seem increasingly threatened by globalization: the expansion of trade liberalization to more and more sectors, the spread of the Internet and other communications technologies, the growing use of the English language as the means for all this communication, and an ever more powerful geopolitical role for the main beneficiary of globalization, the United States. Uncontrolled globalization, many French worry, will oblige France to abandon some of the most distinctive and best-loved aspects of its entertainment, art, culinary traditions, and language—in short, those things that most make it France.[1]

Such concerns are evident in public opinion polls, which reveal that a majority of the French (56 percent) believe that globalization threatens their national identity.[2] Polls also show a particular concern that globalization will come in the form of Americanization: 65 percent of the French see "excessive" U.S. influence on French television, 57 percent on French cinema, 37 percent on French music, 34 percent on the French language, and 34 percent on French food.[3] Polls also suggest that the French are more worried about this than their neighbors: 33 percent of the French surveyed said that U.S. popular culture was a "serious or very serious threat" to their own culture, compared with 27 percent in the United Kingdom, 24 percent in Germany, and 19 percent in Italy.[4] Perhaps surprisingly, given the penetration of American culture (such as music and clothing) among the younger generations, even younger French people seem to share these concerns; no less than 74 percent of French people aged fifteen to twenty-four expressed the view that the influence of American culture in France is "excessive."[5]

In this context it is perhaps not surprising that almost all French politicians support efforts to limit globalization when it comes to issues that affect culture and identity—a policy often referred to as the "cultural exception." Indeed, whereas in the economic arena there is at least some debate across the political spectrum about whether to embrace or to contain globalization (even if the "embracers" are relatively few and quiet), as globalization proceeds, "French politicians have been queuing up to support the right to cultural protectionism," the *Economist* observed in late 1999.[6] This interventionist impulse may result, in part, from the retreat of the French state from its *dirigiste* economic role. Instead of managing the economy, where there is a growing acceptance that its role has been excessive, the French state is now concentrating its efforts in the

areas of social and cultural policies to try to manage the effects of globalization rather than stop it.

However legitimate French concerns about culture and identity, it is
not clear how successful measures to contain the cultural effects of globalization will be. Regulations on the use of the French language are often
mocked, hard to enforce, and usually ignored. McDonald's and other fast-
food restaurants are proliferating despite the government's efforts to promote French gastronomy. And while subsidies for French cinema ensure
that more French films are made, they do not make them widely watched
or exported. Conversely, French culture is probably more resilient than
many French people seem to think, and as long as it has something to
offer, it will not disappear with globalization. Indeed, as we argue in this
chapter, globalization can also be a powerful new means to enrich French
culture and spread it around the world.

French Culture and Identity in Historical Perspective

Globalization in its current incarnation may be causing the latest phase of
French concerns about cultural identity, but the issue has a long history.
Throughout the twentieth century, and in particular during the postwar
period, France has been worried that it is gradually losing its capacity for
cultural influence (*rayonnement*), often to the new global cultural power,
the United States. Concerns about French identity and "Americanization"
started as early as the 1920s, when French writers began to criticize the
rising America's way of life.[7] Georges Duhamel's prominent book, *America
the Menace,* was just one of many in the interwar period that conveyed
the sense that American culture was not only unappealing in itself (which
was America's problem), but, more important, threatened to spread to
France.[8] French journalists, politicians, intellectuals, and other visitors to
the United States worried that America's consumer- and profit-oriented
society, concerned more with "modernity" than with "civilization," would
have a negative impact on France and its own traditions.[9]

Such concerns intensified in the postwar period for three main reasons.
First, economic growth and urbanization dramatically changed the face
of France, leading some to fear for its national identity. Second, America's
role in Europe and throughout the world grew, fueling anti-American sentiment. Third, France was eclipsed by the two superpowers on the global
stage at the same time as it was losing its colonial empire. Except for the
pro-Soviet Communists, the French recognized that the American cultural

threat was less serious than the Soviet military one, but it was nonetheless significant. As political scientist Maurice Duverger put it in *Le Monde* on August 9, 1948, "The American threat remains for the moment less urgent, less serious, and less dangerous than the Soviet menace. . . . Between the invasion of *Gletkins* and the invasion of *Digests*, we certainly prefer the latter; however, in the long run the civilization of *Digests* will kill the European spirit just as surely as the civilization of *Gletkins*."[10]

Already in 1946, the potential for American domination of French cinema was a prominent political issue. As part of the Blum-Byrnes loan negotiations over postwar U.S. economic aid to France, the Americans insisted on an end to the strong protectionist measures to keep the French film market closed—an early version of the *exception culturelle*.[11] Under the accord, the French managed to preserve some level of protection against the onslaught of Hollywood, but not enough to prevent the leader of the French Communist Party, Maurice Thorez, from accusing the government of allowing American films to "poison the souls of French children." Thorez warned that American cinema would not only take jobs away from French artists and musicians, but would turn young French people into the "docile slaves of the American billionaires, and not French boys and girls attached to the moral and intellectual values that have been responsible for the grandeur and glory of our homeland."[12] Notwithstanding the communist rhetoric, his words serve as a good reminder that the current debate about American cinema is neither new nor, by historical standards, particularly vitriolic.

The arrival of large volumes of American-made consumer products—referred to at the time by the French press as "coca-colonization"—was also seen as a threat to French identity. As with the movie industry, the perceived threat from Coca-Cola contained an element of simple economic protectionism: winemakers strongly supported the campaign against Coke. Mostly, however, it was the cultural fear of mass-produced American consumer goods flooding the postwar European market. As *Le Monde* warned in 1949, the arrival of Coca-Cola was the beginning of a cultural invasion that would change France: "Chryslers and Buicks speed down our roads; American tractors furrow our fields; Frigidaires keep our food cold; stockings 'made by Du Pont' sheathe the legs of our stylish women."[13] In another comment with striking similarities to the critiques of the invasion of McDonald's in the 1990s, *Le Monde* also claimed that Coca-Cola's "red delivery trucks and walls covered with signs, placards, and advertisements" recalled totalitarian propaganda, by which "whole peoples have been intoxicated. The moral landscape of France is at stake."[14] As Richard Kuisel describes it, the concern, at least for the French elite, was "the danger that America would export its mass culture, threatening the French conception of humanistic and high culture with adulteration by the technical values and products of mass culture. In other words the productivity mania, Coca-Cola, and the *Reader's Digest* were a danger."[15]

In part as a response to such concerns, in 1959 de Gaulle established a powerful Ministry of Culture, headed until 1969 by the writer André Malraux, with a mandate and budget to promote French culture.[16] Malraux expanded the Fourth Republic's policy of subsidizing French films by placing a levy on cinema tickets (to an extent, taxing American films to pay for French ones) and gave new impetus to state-led cultural promotion. One of his primary instruments was the creation of cultural centers called Maisons de la Culture, designed to promote French culture in France.[17] Nevertheless the worries about French identity continued, with analyst Maurice Duverger writing in *L'Express* about the "dangers" of American civilization (now that the Soviet threat had largely receded) and Sorbonne professor René Etiemble denouncing the development of "franglais."[18] The most prominent expression of this concern, however, was Jean-Jacques Servan-Schreiber's 1967 book, *The American Challenge*, which sold over half a million copies in its first three months. While the title sounds like a call to arms, in fact *The American Challenge* was more a call to imitate American practices than to oppose them—and for reasons as much cultural as economic. If Europe did not act quickly to reestablish control over its own economy and society, Servan-Schreiber warned, Europeans might prosper, but they would be "dominated, for the first time in [their] history, by a more advanced civilization." The Americans would eventually control European publishing, press, television, and other cultural industries, and France's "cultural 'messages,'" "customs," and "ways of life and thought" would be "controlled from the outside."[19]

Such concerns abated somewhat in the 1970s as America turned inward in the wake of Vietnam, the energy crisis, and economic recession. Already by the early 1980s, however, François Mitterrand's culture minister, Jack Lang, was boycotting the American film festival at Deauville and railing against the "invasion" of and "subversion" by "foreign images and standardized music . . . that flatten cultures and carry with them a homogenized way of life that some want to impose on the entire planet."[20] Lang also denounced the American television show *Dallas* as an example of cultural imperialism and a threat to French national identity.[21] Under the influence of this popular minister, by 1986 France's culture budget had risen to some 10 billion francs—more than twice the level under President Valéry Giscard d'Estaing and greater as a share of the overall budget than under de Gaulle and Malraux.[22]

Like Malraux two decades previously, Lang sought to use his augmented budgets to promote French culture in a wide range of areas. The 1980s were also marked by another perceived threat to French identity—becoming "Europeanized." The development of the European Community's Single Market program and France's renewed commitment to European integration led some to believe that their French distinctiveness would be dissolved in a wider European melting pot. These concerns gained weight alongside a growing resentment of immigration. Yet to many French, the only way to avoid sacrificing French identity through Americanization was to accept Europeanization, itself a threat to French identity, albeit a lesser one.

To be sure, the 1980s were characterized as much by fascination with and appreciation for Ronald Reagan's America as by the fear of becoming Americanized.[23] Yet these pro-American wave sentiments were not enough to prevent the reemergence of the familiar concerns about American cultural domination in the early 1990s. When "Euro-Disney" (now renamed Disneyland-Paris) opened in 1992, French intellectuals, the media, and many politicians denounced Disney's arrival in France as yet another American threat to French cultural traditions. One French theater director, Ariane Mnouchkine, went so far as to call it a "cultural Chernobyl."[24] By the 1990s, the French were no longer as sensitive as they had been in the 1950s about Americanization, but the Disney episode showed that the old fears were not entirely gone.[25]

Trade and the Challenge to Cultural Identity

French concerns about culture and identity have thus been manifested in cycles of greater or lesser intensity throughout the postwar period. The latest wave of concern stems from the unprecedented openness to outside cultural influences associated with globalization. Globalization is seen as a new threat to culture and identity because it breaks down both the *natural* barriers to external cultural influence via technology (for example, the Internet and developments that lead to falling communication and transportation costs) and the *artificial* barriers, such as trade and investment restrictions, via increasingly open trade that extends deeper and deeper into the national economy and society.

When trade liberalization was limited to certain types of goods and services and was primarily concerned with tariffs and quotas, trade politics essentially revolved around *economic* arguments about jobs and prices. Trade policy could be manipulated to protect special interests, and when governments decided to open up certain economic sectors to international competition, the relevant special interests could be compensated. With each round of multilateral trade negotiations under the General Agreement on Tariffs and Trade (GATT), however, traditional trade barriers have been further reduced and new types of nontariff barriers discussed. During the 1987–93 Uruguay Round, the "new issues" of services and intellectual property were added to the traditional trade agenda. By touching on sectors that were politically sensitive, trade was starting to impinge on national prerogatives and, at the same time, directly affecting definitions of national identity. Subsuming these new issues under the reach of "trade" naturally led to the inclusion of even more sensitive issues, such as food safety and labor laws, for subsequent discussion in international trade forums.

Culture was among the new issues discussed at the Uruguay Round. In 1993, toward the end of the discussions, the United States attempted to apply free trade principles to "cultural goods"—primarily audiovisuals, through a debate over the European Union's broadcasting directive Television without Frontiers. This led to a strong reaction in France, which managed (not without difficulty) to win the support of its European partners to defend the principle of "cultural exception" on the premise that culture was not just another type of merchandise.[26] Despite strong lobbying from Hollywood, Europe successfully resisted U.S. pressure on the cultural issue. President Mitterrand argued that "no country should be allowed to control the images of the whole world," and France managed to preserve the right to subsidize its cultural goods and protect them with quotas.[27] Contrary to what is often assumed, the GATT accord did not explicitly exclude cultural goods from free trade in services, but by failing to explicitly include those goods, it effectively gave the EU the right to do so.

The issue of cultural exception emerged again a few years later in the context of negotiations over the Multilateral Agreement on Investment (MAI). Conceived in 1995 and launched in 1997 in Paris, the MAI negotiations between the twenty-nine members of the Organization for Economic Cooperation and Development (OECD) were designed to establish rules governing investment, in the same way that GATT, and later the

World Trade Organization (WTO), established rules for free trade.[28] One of the consequences of the draft agreement would have been to render illegal regulations protecting cultural investments in Europe (which the French had prevented the 1993 Uruguay Round agreement from doing). Consumer groups in the United States and Canada publicized the draft text and launched an international campaign protesting the negotiations. Under the leadership of Jack Lang, the French entertainment sector also mobilized against the MAI, which was scheduled to be signed in April 1998. Just as in the GATT negotiations, French movie directors, actors, and musicians raised public awareness about the dangers of subjecting culture to the imperatives of global capital. Eventually, they got their message across to the politicians, who pulled France out of the negotiations, triggering their collapse.

The defeat of the MAI, although the result of lack of agreement on a broad set of issues, was the first real victory of the French antiglobalization camp. It was also the first successful alliance between the cultural sector and other segments of the French society—for example, between intellectuals and farmers. While this alliance built on well-established elements in the repertoire of political mobilization in France—such as the communist tradition of alliance between intellectuals and manual workers—the defense of France's culture against globalization proved to be a particularly strong force for bringing these diverse groups together.

Because of the evolving nature of trade during the 1990s, the French debate on the benefits and problems of free trade has shifted from the economic to the political and cultural realms. When the United States and the EU argued over the issue of cultural exception at the end of the Uruguay Round in 1993, the debate was limited to cultural goods narrowly defined—movies, music, and television programming. What has changed in recent years is the realization that the threat to French culture comes not only from trade in cultural goods, but more broadly from trade in general; a movie by Eric Rohmer, after all, is no more a defining component of French cultural identity than foie gras or Parisian cafés—and all seem threatened by globalization.

The Entertainment Sector

Some of the greatest debates about the cultural effects of globalization concern the entertainment sector, primarily cinema and television. The extent of the domination of those American industries in France, and in

Europe more widely, is striking. According to the European Audiovisual Observatory, the EU market for U.S. audiovisual goods broadly defined (including movie ticket sales, videocassette rentals, and television rights) in 1998 was $7.4 billion, compared with a U.S. market for European audiovisual goods of just $706 million.[29] The deficit, moreover, has been growing since the end of the 1980s, when it was only around $2 billion (1988). Between 1985 and 1999, the U.S. share of the average EU market in movie ticket sales rose from 56 percent to 70 percent.[30] By contrast, the U.S. market apparently continues to be largely impenetrable: just 1–2 percent of films shown in the United States are translated from a foreign language, and hardly any continental European productions appear on American television.[31]

Music and books also show strong international, and particularly American, influence, albeit to a lesser degree. As of 1996, 48 percent of the music played on French radio stations was French, a national proportion slightly higher than for other European countries.[32] This relatively high national share was largely due to the 1994 Toubon law mandating a 40 percent quota of French-language songs on French radio stations during prime listening time (between 5:30 a.m. and 10:30 p.m.); before the Toubon law, 80 percent of popular music on French radio was American or British.[33] In August 2000 a new audiovisual law introduced some flexibility in the French-language requirement, allowing the quota to drop to 35 percent in certain cases and changing the quotas for songs by new artists, but the principle that the state should intervene to preserve the French cultural heritage and to ensure ongoing cultural creation in French remained.

As for books, as of the 1990s less than a quarter of those published in most of the major European countries were translated works—14 percent in Germany, 17 percent in France, 25 percent in Italy, and 26 percent in Spain—though these figures tend to understate the real impact of foreign books, since among bestsellers the proportion of translated works is normally higher. Of books translated into French, more than 45 percent were of American origin and 30 percent were British. Again, European rates of foreign penetration contrasted sharply with the United States, where only 3 percent of published books were translated (of course, this does not take account of British imports).[34]

In France, the area of greatest concern within the entertainment sector is cinema. Thanks in part to large government subsidies and other forms of protection for movie producers, the French movie industry is faring much better than any other in Europe. After a decline in the early 1990s,

France now produces 100 to 150 full-length features annually (more if one counts coproductions), which is far more than in either Germany or Italy.[35] In 1999, French movies captured about 38 percent of domestic ticket sales, compared with 24 percent for Italian movies in Italy, 18 percent for British movies in the United Kingdom, 14 percent for German movies in Germany, and 10 percent for Spanish films in Spain.[36] With respect to television screening—arguably more important in terms of cultural influence, because it reaches larger audiences—the French are also faring better than other European countries, but they are not entirely resisting American domination. Foreign films take a 35–39 percent share of the market on the main French television stations, compared with 43–85 percent in Germany; 62–77 percent in Spain; 60–84 percent in Britain; and 52–71 percent in Italy.[37]

Nevertheless, the French movie sector continues to be dominated by American exports. As shown in table 3-1, in 2000 a French film (*Taxi 2*) was the top box office draw, and two others (*Le Goût des Autres* and *Les Rivières Pourpres*) made it into the top ten. Overall, however, French films took only a 28.5 percent share of ticket sales in France that year, compared with 62.9 percent for American films.[38] In 1999 a French coproduction, *Astérix et Obélix,* was the top box office draw in France, but the eight next biggest successes in that year were American (or in two cases, Anglo-American) films: *Tarzan, Star Wars, Matrix, Notting Hill, The World Is Not Enough, The Mummy, A Bug's Life,* and *Wild, Wild West.* Of the forty most successful films in France in 1999, twenty-six were American and seven French (plus three French coproductions). Moreover, while increasing numbers of French movies are being *made* (rising from 95 in 1995 to 148 in 1998 and 181 in 1999), they are not necessarily being *seen.* In 1998, for example, three French films (*Le Dîner de Cons, Les Visiteurs 2,* and *Taxi*) were among the top four movies in ticket sales in France, surpassed only by the American *Titanic*; but those three films alone accounted for no less than 45 percent of the total revenues from the 148 French movies made that year. No other French film made it into the top fifty.[39]

Even these figures are exaggerated, since many movie makers take advantage of the flexible rules on what is "French" in order to get access to French subsidies. Examples of this include the 1995 Milos Forman film *Valmont,* which counted as "French" even though it was a Franco-British coproduction, shot in English, with seven American and two British actors; and Roland Joffé's 1999 Franco-American coproduction *Vatel,* which

Table 3-1.   *Top Ten Box Office Films in France, 1998–2000*

Rank	1998	1999	2000
1	Titanic (U.S.)	Astérix et Obélix (France, Germany, Italy)	Taxi 2 (France)
2	Le Dîner de Cons (France)	Tarzan (U.S.)	The Sixth Sense (U.S.)
3	Les Couloirs du Temps—Les Visiteurs II (France)	Star Wars: Episode 1—The Phantom Menace (U.S.)	Dinosaur (U.S.)
4	Taxi (France)	Matrix (U.S.)	Gladiator (U.S.)
5	Mulan (U.S.)	Notting Hill (U.K., U.S.)	Toy Story 2 (U.S.)
6	Armageddon (U.S.)	The World Is Not Enough (U.K., U.S.)	MI-2: Mission Impossible (U.S.)
7	La Vita è bella (Italy)	The Mummy (U.S.)	Le Goût des Autres (France)
8	Saving Private Ryan (U.S.)	A Bug's Life (U.S.)	Scary Movie (U.S.)
9	Prince of Egypt (U.S.)	Wild, Wild West (U.S.)	Unbreakable (U.S.)
10	There's Something about Mary (U.S.)	Jeanne d'Arc (France)	Les Rivières Pourpres (France)

Source: Ciné Box-Office (www.cinebox-office.com); and Observatoire européen de l'audiovisuel, *Statistical Yearbook 2000* (Strasbourg, 2000).

was shot in English and starred an American actress.[40] Indeed, seeking to reach a wider audience, more and more French filmmakers are also starting to film in English, for example, Luc Besson, with his recent film, *The Messenger: The Story of Joan of Arc*.[41] In the face of such globalization in the film industry, it is becoming harder to attribute a nationality to a movie.[42]

To defend their domestic production, the French—pulling the Europeans along when possible—have resorted to a variety of protectionist measures for what they define as cultural goods. At France's urging, for example, the European Union included measures to support the European film industry in its 1989 television broadcasting directive, Television without Frontiers (an ironic title, since from a non-European perspective it was about television *with* frontiers).[43] The directive requires that "when practicable" the major proportion of television time be devoted to transmissions of European origin (excluding news, sports, and advertisements), with "European" defined for films as those originating in Europe, made mainly by authors and workers residing in Europe, and for coproductions as those in which Europeans exercise "preponderant" control.[44] Some countries are more rigorous than others in enforcing the directive (indeed many get away with broadcasting a large proportion of their European quotas at times when few people are watching), but France has chosen to impose even stricter regulations—60 percent of transmissions must be European and 50 percent must be in the French language—and to apply narrower definitions of what constitutes a European production.

The French are also much more aggressive than others in defending their movie industry. Their main tool is a 10 percent cinema tax (in practice, to a large extent a tax on American films, given their domination of the market), the revenue from which is used to subsidize French productions. These subsidies may take any of three forms: an advance before the film is made, an advance for distribution, or aid for improvement of the script. Films are eligible if they are shot in French using "predominantly French" personnel, and grant decisions are based either on the results of the producer's previous film (*aide automatique*) or on an assessment of the "quality" of the film after an initial reading of the script by a group of directors, actors, writers, producers, and critics (*commission de l'avance sur recette*).[45] The average subsidy per film is currently 2 million francs. Of the 181 films produced in France in 1999, only three were able to cover costs at the French box office.[46]

Why are the French willing to go to such extremes—incurring clear economic costs, ruffling feathers with some of their European partners, and provoking major trade disputes with the United States—in order to defend their national audiovisual industries? To an extent, support for subsidies for French cinema are based on the perception of an uneven playing field and the view that market failure needs to be corrected. Foreign Minister Hubert Védrine, for example, defends the widespread view that cultural goods cannot be "treated, produced, exchanged, and sold like any other," and points to the "vast internal market" and "huge resources" that enable Hollywood to "flood markets abroad."[47] Former culture minister Lang adds that "the traditional market system cannot always assure the necessary financing" to keep French cinema in business, and other analysts, such as Laurent Burin des Roziers, point to Americans' control of distribution channels, massive marketing budgets, and unwillingness to show subtitled films as reasons for their domination.[48] All of these arguments are widely accepted in France and contain more than an element of truth.

Yet the *main* argument for protecting the French audiovisual industry is not economic or commercial but cultural. Indeed, even many who would

agree with what *Libération's* film critic has called the "unpleasant truth"—
that "the average American film [might be] better than the average French
film"—believe that French cinema should be defended, in order to preserve what is unique about French identity and culture and to preserve
cultural diversity in France and for the world.[49] In fact, since the mid-
1990s the French have started talking a lot less about the "cultural exception" and more about "cultural diversity," a more positive way of looking
at the need to defend French culture in an age of globalization.[50] According to Catherine Trautmann, Jospin's culture minister from 1997 to 2000,
"cultural exception is the legal tool, cultural diversity is the goal."[51]

Ultimately, the defense of French cinema and other visual arts is largely
a public goods argument: diversity benefits the French and the world as a
whole, so the government must step in to correct a market failure. In
doing so, France claims to act for the benefit of the world at large by
bringing into existence worthwhile movies that would otherwise be unlikely to get produced. In Védrine's words, the "desire to preserve cultural
diversity in the world is in no way a sign of anti-Americanism but of anti-
hegemony. It's a rejection of impoverishment. American cinema has been
enchanting viewers around the world for nearly a century, and that will
continue. This is no reason for others to disappear."[52]

Food

Food is another area in which the French government has stepped in to
counter market forces in the name of the preservation of cultural diversity. Of all the components of French cultural identity, food may be one of
the most widely recognized throughout the world and one of the greatest
sources of pride at home. Consequently, perceived threats to that source
of pride are taken very seriously. As Jean-Michel Normand has argued in
Le Monde, "McDonald's . . . commercial hegemony threatens our agriculture and its cultural hegemony insidiously ruins alimentary behavior—
both sacred reflections of the French identity." "Resistance to the
hegemonic pretenses of hamburgers," Alain Rollat agrees, "is, above all, a
cultural imperative."[53] The huge success of Jean-Pierre Coffe, who has
made a career—through books and a highly popular television show—of
defending French culinary traditions against *la malbouffe,* is another indication of how seriously the French public takes the issue.[54]

According to its critics, fast food, in particular, embodies globalization
in its culinary dimension. It is a one-size-fits-all approach to food, encour-

aging uniformity and playing on the lowest common denominator of tastes. As such, it is the direct opposite of French culinary traditions. The mayor of one small village in southwestern France sums up this position: "Roquefort is made from the milk of only one breed of sheep, it is made in only one place in France, and it is made in only one special way. It is the opposite of globalization. Coca-Cola you can buy anywhere in the world and it is exactly the same. Coke is a symbol of the American multinationals that want to uniformize taste all over the planet. That's what we're against."[55]

Fast food has also become a symbolic target of antiglobalization protesters because of its American origin. According to French sociologist Michel Crozier, "For many French people there is an association that good food is French and fast food is American and foreign and bad."[56] The French agriculture minister, Jean Glavany, expressed this view by declaring to the press in June 1999 that the United States has "the worst food in the world" and publicly announcing in August that he had never eaten at McDonald's and disliked hamburgers.[57] Indeed, French sociologist Jean-Pierre Poulain notes, "During my field research, I have been struck by the strange self-justification discourse used by most adults, saying that they were coming to McDonald's for the first and last time. It was as if they were coming out of an X-rated movie."[58]

Particularly distressing for the defenders of French culinary tradition is the enormous surge of popularity that fast food is enjoying in France. While the number of traditional brasseries and cafés has fallen from some 200,000 in 1960 to around 50,000 today, the number of fast food and takeout businesses has doubled from 6,500 in 1993 to 13,950 in 1998.[59] As of March 2000, McDonald's alone had nearly 800 outlets in France, with a total revenue of around 10 billion francs. The culinary profession contends, not entirely without reason, that this popularity is in part due to domestic tax laws: meals in French restaurants are burdened with a 19.6 percent value added tax (reduced from 20.6 percent in spring 2000), whereas the tax rate for takeout fast food is only 5.5 percent.[60] Clearly, however, there are other explanations for the expansion of fast food in France—including cost, convenience, marketing, service, and even the fact that many people appear to like it.[61]

In ways that parallel the efforts to preserve a national entertainment industry, the French government has taken steps to ensure the defense of the country's gastronomical patrimony. In 1989 the Ministry of Culture created the Conseil National des Arts Culinaires (National Council of

Culinary Arts), with a mission to protect French gastronomy. Among its various programs are "taste education" for schoolchildren, designed to train their palates to be more sophisticated, and the "inventory" and promotion of the culinary patrimony of each region of France.[62] This state intervention in the food sector raises some of the same questions as does intervention in the entertainment industry. Why does the state feel compelled to protect its citizens from their free will? The McDonald's on the Champs Elysées, after all, is the most frequently patronized "restaurant" in all of France, and the crowds that gather there daily are far from all foreigners. Why do the French support the government's efforts even when they seem to run counter to their own tastes?

One reason why the French approve of a collective struggle against McDonald's, even if they patronize its outlets, is their belief in the value of cultural diversity. The rationale is not to get rid of McDonald's, but to ensure that it does not entirely displace traditional French restaurants and culinary traditions. As is the case for movies, pure market forces can have a homogenizing effect and tend to limit variety. The number of cultivated varieties of fruits and vegetables has dwindled considerably over the years, not only in France but everywhere in the world, as farmers have flocked toward the highest yielding, most disease resistant, and easiest to transport varieties (in the United States, one sees a reaction to this process in the movement for "heirloom" vegetables). There is a widespread belief in France today that the same kind of homogenization should not happen in gastronomy, the diversity of which is an essential component of French culture. As French historian René Rémond explains, "the crusade against *la malbouffe* is the transposition of George Duhamel's argument in *America the Menace*, defending French artisans against American mass production."[63]

Adversaries of globalization also argue that it represents a threat to French "gastronomical sovereignty," not only because it homogenizes tastes but also because it puts consumer health at risk. Mad cow disease (bovine spongiform encephalopathy, or BSE), which can potentially cause brain disease in humans, and other recent food scares have made food safety a top priority. BSE broke out in British livestock in 1996, and despite the slaughter of animals and a ban on British beef exports to other European countries, the disease was subsequently discovered elsewhere, including in France. By 2000, public concern over mad cow disease was extremely high and the disease had become one of the top political issues in the country. Several other crises added to this sense of insecurity about food.

For instance, in 1999 it was revealed that Belgian animal feed (especially used for poultry) was tainted with cancer-causing dioxin. This scandal had implications well beyond Belgian borders, since the tainted feed was sold to farmers in France and the Netherlands. In the same year, French authorities recalled all canned drinks manufactured by Coca-Cola (50 million cans of Coca-Cola, Diet Coke, Sprite, and Fanta) pulled off store shelves after 200 people reported feeling ill after drinking Coca-Cola products.

Globalization is blamed for these food scares for several reasons. First, as a result of trade openness in agricultural goods, France has no control over what comes across its borders. As José Bové puts it, "all of a sudden we realized that globalization could oblige us to ingest hormones."[64] This is why, when the WTO ruled in 1999 that the European Union could not ban imports of hormone-treated beef, the EU was willing to face U.S. sanctions rather than go against the will of its citizens and accept such products, unlabeled, on European markets. Concern over genetically modified foods is also widespread in France, although apparently less so than in other European countries. According to recent polls, 24 percent of French say they would "never" eat a genetically modified food even if it were tested and approved by government and industry experts—well short of the Germans (46 percent), Austrians (44 percent), Italians (44 percent), and British (33 percent).[65] The discrepancy could reflect the fact that while the French are indeed skeptical of genetically modified foods, they have more confidence in their state to effectively test and approve foods.

Second, critics such as Bové and the Confédération Paysanne argue that the new food safety crises are a consequence of the industrialization of agriculture.[66] Instead of the direct link that used to exist between the farmer and the consumer, agriculture is now part of an industrial chain. The farmers become the employees of large agribusiness companies that control the processing and distribution of foodstuffs. As a result, food production is dominated by a race for profit, leading farmers to use some unorthodox (and potentially dangerous) methods—such as feeding herbivorous cattle with animal carcasses and depleting the soil through the intensive use of chemicals.

A third criticism is that because of globalization, food is no longer produced locally. It therefore becomes necessary to resort to technology to ensure that it can travel the ever-growing distances between producers and consumers and arrive in good condition. As a result of the globalization of the food chain, food contains more preservatives—and tastes worse.[67] Even though French consumers buy such products, they worry about them and would rather have their government apply the "precautionary principle" (a concept allowing governments to block imports on public safety grounds) whenever possible. As *Le Figaro* puts it, "what most bothers the French is that decisions about their health are taken by big companies or by far-away institutions, without those decisions being fully explained."[68] The French reaction to the WTO ruling on hormone-treated beef and the clear opposition to genetically modified food must be understood in this context.

Responses to the portrayal of globalization as a direct attack on French food identity have come on many fronts. In 1999, for the first time since the introduction of fast food in France, fast food à la française (baguette sandwiches from French chains) outnumbered burger outlets, including McDonald's and European brands, such as Quick.[69] As for McDonald's, it has felt compelled to respond to the general climate of mistrust. In fall 1999, McDonald's France ran a large-scale advertising campaign built around the slogan "Born in the United States. Made in France." The ads emphasized that the ingredients used were indeed French and, in particular, that the beef was free both of hormones (from the United States) and BSE (from Britain).[70] And in spring 2000, McDonald's launched locally themed meals. In March it ran a promotion in which customers could buy a burger topped with a different variety of French cheese on each day of the week. In April it offered "gourmet" menus in the South of France, including burgers topped with ratatouille, and black currant ice cream for dessert. This is part of a strategy based on lessons learned from other American companies, including Disney, that American "cultural" exports go over best when adapted in some way to French culture.[71]

Language and the Francophonie

Globalization is also a threat because it strengthens the role of the English language—in part at the expense of the French language, a prominent component of French identity.[72] Indeed, many French people would agree with Maurice Druon, until recently perpetual secretary general of the Académie Francaise, that "the language of a people is its soul."[73] Foreign Minister Védrine argues that the French language is "vital to French identity" and does not accept that it would "somehow be 'old-fashioned' to defend it." "Our language," he asserts, is "like our genetic code."[74] The Conseil Supérieur de la Langue Française (High Council for the French

Language), presided over by the prime minister (see below), adds that "French is at the heart of our culture and of our heritage."[75] And for former French culture minister Jacques Toubon, the French language is nothing less than the "primary capital" of the French people, "the symbol of their dignity, the passageway to integration [and] part of the French dream."[76]

Language is particularly important to France for several reasons. First, it is one of the central unifying, republican forces in France, the "cement of the republic and the values it is founded on," in the words of Prime Minister Jospin.[77] It is for this reason that in June 1992 the French parliament amended the constitution to specify that "the language of the Republic is French."[78] This was intended not only as a protective measure against the intrusion of foreign words, but also against the growing popularity of some minority and regional languages (such as Breton, Corsican, Alsatian, Occitan, and others). Similarly, France for years remained the only country in Western Europe to refuse to sign the Charter on Regional and Minority Languages passed by the Council of Europe in 1992. After the Jospin government had negotiated certain clarifications designed to protect the position of French as the national language, France finally signed the charter in 1999, but President Chirac challenged its constitutionality. In June 1999 the Constitutional Council deemed the charter incompatible with article 2 of the French constitution ("The language of the Republic is French"), making its ratification by parliament, which would thus require a constitutional amendment, unlikely.[79] "Throughout its history," one expert has written, "the linguistic unification of France has been linked to its political unification and to the progress of centralization."[80]

Second, language is closely associated with a country's stature and influence in the world, and France still seeks both. The French realize that theirs is no longer the international language of diplomacy, treaties, and nobility that it once was, but they want to preserve as much of their former influence as possible. As Jospin put it, "French is no longer the language of a power [but] it could be a language of counterpower."[81]

Finally, the French justify their need to defend their language in the same way as they justify all other aspects of their identity: as a necessary contribution to diversity throughout the world. In the words of Boutros Boutros-Ghali, secretary general of the Francophonie (the organization set up in 1986 to promote the French language), the defense of French is a "fight to make sure that globalization does not become a synonym for uniformization and that the respect of cultural and linguistic diversity becomes the main force for a true democracy on a global scale."[82] Likewise, the official statement of a March 2001 conference held in Paris and attended by Jacques Chirac argued that "the forces of uniformity created by the new realities of globalization require an activist approach by the states."[83] To cite Jospin once again, "French can become one of the languages in which the resistance to uniformity in the world is expressed, the refusal of identities to fade, the encouragement of freedom to create and to express oneself in one's own culture. It is in this respect that France wants to be the motor of cultural diversity in the world."[84]

Concern for the future of the French language is nothing new. L'Académie Française, dedicated to the defense of language and culture, was created by Cardinal de Richelieu in 1635, with the sole obligation "to give clear rules to our language and make it pure, eloquent, and capable of handling the arts and the sciences."[85] Today the job of the forty *académiciens,* with an average age of well over seventy, includes keeping the language "pure" by protecting it from excessive foreign influences. In 1883—in part to overcome the loss of prestige suffered in the 1870–71 Franco-Prussian War—the French government created the Alliance Française to promote the teaching of French language and literature in colonies and elsewhere. The idea, according to one analyst, was that "as foreigners grew more familiar with the French intellectual tradition, they would come to sympathize with French economic and political policies. The projection of French culture abroad thus became a significant component of French diplomacy."[86] In 1986 the Organisation Internationale de la Francophonie was set up as yet another tool to promote French language and culture around the world. It now includes fifty-five member states, has nine candidate members, and has an annual budget of 1 billion francs. It pursues its goals through a variety of means, including providing support for the teaching of French, running a French-only TV channel that broadcasts worldwide, developing cultural exchange, and facilitating cultural creation in French. The Francophonie, which meets regularly in an international summit (for example, in Hanoi, Vietnam, in 1997; Moncton, Canada, in 1999; and Beirut, Lebanon, in 2001), is also active in defense of the use of French in international diplomacy, where it was once predominant but is now used less and less.[87]

More controversially, France has sometimes resorted to legislation to defend its language. In December 1975 the Bas-Lauriol law made French mandatory in all written and spoken advertising, instructions on packages, and official documents. It also banned the use of foreign words when French alternatives are available. In August 1994, the Bas-Lauriol law was updated by the Toubon law, named for Culture Minister Jacques Toubon (who as justice minister in 1997 called the spread of English "a new form of colonization"). The Toubon law mandated fines or even prison sentences if French was not used in advertisements and public announcements. It also banned all public subsidies for scientific conferences not held in French. The Constitutional Council weakened the first draft of the law on freedom of expression grounds, allowing only clauses decreeing that employment contracts and instructions on pharmaceutical containers and machinery must be in French or carry a full translation, but the final version of the law is still far-reaching.[88]

The Toubon law has been actively applied. The Body Shop, for example, was among several dozen companies fined for using English to advertise or label its products in 1996.[89] In 1998 the law resulted in nearly 8,000 linguistic inspections, 658 warnings, 255 cases brought before the public prosecutor, and 124 successful prosecutions.[90] The Toubon law has been widely derided, both inside and outside France, but the fact that it was passed shows the extent of the concern for the future of the French language. Former culture minister Jack Lang, not known for shying from the defense of French culture, opposed the law on the grounds that "excess Franglais may be absurd, but to ban it is dictatorship, and more absurd."[91] Védrine, however, has said that he finds "more to be said for the Toubon law . . . than against it."[92] Védrine also worries that American English might become a "predatory language that will progressively smother an entire series of other languages in countries where everyone will learn American because it is too archaic, absurd, provincial and chauvinistic not to speak American."[93]

In November 1999 the French government created the Conseil Supérieur de la Langue Française, an agency under the direct control of the prime minister that would be in charge of studying the practice, enrichment, and promotion of the French language.[94] In March 2000 the Ministry of Finance announced that it had banned many common English business words, including *e-mail* and *start-up*. Instead, civil servants and employees of state-run enterprises are now required to use the terms *courrier électronique* and *jeune-pousse*—the result of months of brainstorming by seven different committees appointed by the ministry in 1999 to provide acceptable translations of as many English computer terms as possible. Although mocked by many, those in charge of the project insist they are simply trying to preserve the purity of the French language. As Jean Saint-Geours, president of the translation team at the Ministry of the Economy, has put it, "I am not an ayatollah on these matters; I'm a pragmatic person. . . . I can't impose these words, but nothing stops me from trying to influence people."[95]

Despite these efforts, English is continuing its progress, and has clearly become the primary language of international business, diplomacy, the Internet, and even, to a large extent, culture. French—with 131 million speakers—is now in ninth place on the list of the world's most widely spoken languages, behind not only English (594 million speakers) but also Spanish, Arabic, and Portuguese. As a first language, French ranks even lower, at eleventh in the world, with 70 million speakers.[96]

In recognition of this reality, the Jospin government, alongside defending the use of French in the world, has actually been trying to promote English as a second working language in France. The current thinking, strongly advocated by Claude Allègre (education minister in 1997–99), is that it is futile to try to stem the tide of English, and so the French might as well learn it better. Allègre also attempted to encourage French researchers to seek a wider audience by delivering and publishing their papers in English rather than in French, but this was seen as a step too far, and he had to retreat quickly.[97] Still, English is now becoming so dominant in French secondary education that specialists are worried about what *Le Monde* has called the "homogenization" of language training in French schools. With nearly 90 percent of French secondary school students choosing English as their first foreign language, Education Ministry officials concede that it is no longer a question of "fighting for diversity of demand in terms of the first language" but of "maintaining diversification of the second."[98]

French is battling English in another arena: international air traffic control. In March 2000 Air France announced that its pilots would henceforth be required to communicate exclusively in English with air traffic controllers at Charles-de-Gaulle international airport in Paris. As this was one of Europe's three busiest airports, it was deemed safer for all communications to be in English, even between a French-speaking crew and a French-speaking control tower, so as to allow all the other pilots to understand the exchange. This measure outraged many Air France employees, however, because it was interpreted as further evidence that France was surrendering to the tide of English. As a result, two weeks after the measure was implemented, Air France was forced to suspend the policy.[99]

Conclusion

The effects of globalization on France's cultural identity are undeniable. Because market forces make globalization tend toward the homogenization of products, and eventually tastes, globalization does threaten some central elements of French national culture. It is therefore not surprising that the French public clings to the notion that the state should offer cultural protection, especially at a time when France seems to have accepted that the state must gradually withdraw from the management of the economy. The French reaction against globalization reflects, to a large extent, nostalgia for a disappearing way of life—when France was an international cultural and political leader. It reflects a feeling of powerlessness in the face of global forces—which activists such as Bové are trying to counter by taking matters into their own hands. It also reflects the fact that, as with all economic, social, and political change, globalization produces "losers," whose products are displaced by those made available through global rather than local markets; the losses sometimes include local traditions and goods. Finally, it reflects the internal contradictions felt by many French men and women, in whom resentment against the perverse effects of globalization coexists with recognition of its positive accomplishments.

Globalization will not necessarily erode French identity, however, and while their efforts to protect it are understandable, the French are probably more sensitive than they need to be. As Arthur Isak Applbaum has written, "there is something worse than to be exiled from one's culture, and that is to be imprisoned by it."[100] While the argument that globalization homogenizes tastes and erases cultural borders is valid, it has a more positive counterpart that is often overlooked: globalization also enables a freer flow of cultures and traditions throughout the world.[101] McDonald's, Coca-Cola, and Mickey Mouse may well have invaded the cultural space of nearly every country in the world, but the *rayonnement* of French culture has also benefited from globalization. In the case of food, for example, globalization has not only meant fast food and hormones in beef but has also greatly expanded the variety of foods—from sushi to Tex-Mex—that can now be consumed in France. French gastronomy, moreover, is now present everywhere in the world. In the United States and the United Kingdom, for instance, many highly rated restaurants have French chefs and offer foods inspired by French cuisine, and cheaper, simpler French "bistrots" have become ubiquitous. American supermarkets now carry a wide variety of French cheeses, going beyond the traditional brie, and sometimes even French gourmet specialty items, such as duck confit and foie gras. In this sense, globalization is not eroding part of French culture, but "growing the franchise," as Theodore C. Bestor has put it.[102]

Likewise for French fashion and luxury goods: Americans can now buy cosmetics at the French chain Sephora on Fifth Avenue in New York, order clothing online from the French mail-order company La Redoute, furnish their homes in Provençal fabrics, and order French wines over the Internet. With the internationalization of the movie business, the French are even having a cultural impact on parts of the world film industry that do not officially count as "French" (and do not get French subsidies). These new possibilities for the spread of French culture are also products of globalization.

The same can be said of language. In the long run it is hard to believe that the French language will be irretrievably polluted by foreign words. The foreign words will blend in—as so many French words have done in other languages, not the least, English. English is no less English because it includes the words *restaurant* or *fuselage,* and there is no reason why French will be any the less French if one says *mél* instead of *courrier électronique* or *start-up* instead of *jeune-pousse.* For decades, the Fontainebleau-based business school, INSEAD, insisted that all its MBA candidates speak French, even though that precluded a number of top students—who might already have been fluent in Japanese, English, Mandarin, German, and Spanish. When it abandoned the French language prerequisite in 1996, INSEAD was not undermining French but no doubt encouraging more international students to study in France, thereby ultimately enhancing the use of French in the world. Even the venerable Institut d'Etudes Politiques de Paris, also known as Sciences Po, has transformed its curriculum to require students to learn and even attend courses in two foreign languages, as well as spend a year abroad. As Dominique Moïsi has written, "The American-accented brand of English is the closest thing we have to a universal language, while the French . . . erect protective linguistic barriers, not understanding that this isolates them instead of preserving their culture. What France should seek to preserve—once it has conceded defeat in the language battle—is the context and originality of its message, not its medium."[103]

The Internet offers another good example of how globalization can cut both ways. While it is true that English is used on an overwhelming majority of Internet web pages (78.3 percent) and that French is very far behind (1.2 percent), the French are finally taking advantage of the Internet boom, and even this small window could be enough to provide access to French ideas, texts, information, and culture all around the world.[104] Even the Académie Française can now be consulted online (www.academie-francaise.fr).[105] And as Reginald Dale has pointed out, "half of the hits on the Internet site of the French newspaper *Libération* come from outside France, suggesting that the Internet is enabling large numbers of people who could not do so before to keep in touch with French news and cultural developments."[106]

In the end, people will only learn French if there is a reason to do so—if French culture, society, and science have something to offer. Similarly, protection and subsidies can help to guarantee that artists will still create works with "French content," but they cannot guarantee quality, or that such works will be "consumed." Given the attraction of France as a tourist destination (75 million tourists visited France in 2000, the most of any country in the world),[107] it is fair to assume that French culture and heritage still have a lot to offer. French culture and identity have proven their resilience and capacity to adapt in the past. As Jean-François Revel has put it, "For French culture to be squashed by Mickey Mouse . . . it would have to be disturbingly fragile."[108] We do not believe that is so.

CHAPTER FOUR

Domestic Politics
and Public
Opinion

"[The attitude of the protesters] stems from the uncertainties globalization creates. . . . This is understandable, and in any case, we've got to take it into account."
Jacques Chirac, after the antiglobalization protests
at the G-8 summit in Genoa, July 2001

Globalization is not only transforming the French economy and affecting French culture, but it is also reshaping the French political system. Globalization alters some of the most basic features of a country's politics, including the relationship between the state and the individual, the expression of cultural identity, and the ways in which democracy is practiced. It redefines the limits of national sovereignty, alters democratic accountability and legitimacy, and upsets the prevailing balance among interest groups and political forces.[1] Thus in France today, some of the traditional cleavages separating the Left from the Right—religion, capitalism, communism, public ownership, education, and so forth—are giving way to, or at least being supplemented by, new divisions and alignments driven by the consequences of globalization.

To be sure, the basic party structure of the Fifth Republic continues, and it is still broadly accurate to talk about "the Left" (Communists, Socialists, and Greens) and "the Right" (liberals, Gaullists, and the extreme Right). But globalization is helping to realign these movements and contributing to what French political analyst Eddy Fougier has called the "mixing up of traditional political-ideological categories."[2] In the debate about globalization, as in the debate about Europe in the early 1990s, the two extremes have more in common with each other than with the center. Communists, Greens, civic movements, and the Socialist left wing stand together with the National Front (NF) and some on the right wing of the Gaullists in their staunch opposition to globalization, while mainstream Socialists, centrists, and moderate Gaullists agree on the need to accept and manage it. Only a small contingent of liberals, backed by the business community, enthusiastically embrace the free flow of goods, people, capital, and ideas associated with globalization and remain relaxed about its potential cultural or geopolitical implications. Also striking is the degree to which globalization has unleashed new forces—from vocal chief executives of privatized companies to activist nongovernmental organizations (NGOs)—that are wielding more influence than ever before in a country where the state has traditionally played the dominant role.

Only a minority of the French in fact oppose globalization and want to reverse it (or believe that it can be reversed). The opponents of globalization wield significant political influence, however, because of the intensity of their feelings and their political activism. Moreover, their main concerns about globalization—that it threatens French identity, creates economic inequalities, or undermines France's geopolitical standing—are shared by many of those who believe globalization is both inevitable and largely beneficial. These factors also explain why French political leaders must tread so carefully as they move—for example, by liberalizing the French economy and limiting the role of the French state—to adapt to the requirements of globalization. In a country where people still look to the state to protect their interests and provide solutions to their problems, it is difficult for that state to tell the people there is little it can do in the face of global markets and trends.

The French Political Spectrum in the Postwar Era

During the Fourth Republic, which lasted from 1946 to 1958, the French political spectrum was divided into three main parts: the French Communist Party (PCF), which was staunchly pro-Soviet, anticapitalist, and anti-American; a centrist "Third Force" made up of Socialists (in the Section Française de l'Internationale Ouvrière, or SFIO), "radicals," and Christian Democrats (the Mouvement Républicain Populaire, or MRP); and, until 1951, the Gaullist Rassemblement pour la France (RPF), which was strongly nationalist and was built around the personality of General de Gaulle. The Third Force, which formed the governments that led France during this period, was diverse in both ideology and makeup. The anti-clerical Socialists strongly disagreed with the largely Catholic MRP on religion, for example, and with both the more business-oriented radicals and the MRP on economic management. But the Socialists and the MRP had other things in common: strong opposition to communism, support for European integration, aversion to de Gaulle, and perhaps most impor-tant, a desire to see the Fourth Republic survive.[3]

Belying the later Gaullist myth of the Fourth Republic as an unmiti-gated disaster, the successive Third Force governments had some impor-tant successes during the 1950s, notably strong economic growth, Franco-German reconciliation, European integration, and the successful transformation of a largely agricultural economy to an industrial and ser-vice-oriented one. Indeed, in retrospect this period might be seen as the successful adaptation to an earlier form of globalization, as trade barriers fell, immigration rose, and outside political and cultural influences prolif-erated. Ultimately, the major geopolitical challenges of the era—the cold war and the struggles over decolonization in Indochina and especially Alge-ria—were too much for the Fourth Republic's weak political structures and coalition governments and brought the regime down in 1958. But in assessing France's confrontation with the major challenge of globaliza-tion today, the country's far-reaching internal transformation in the face of external influences in the 1950s should not be forgotten.[4]

The Fourth Republic was replaced in 1958 by the Fifth Republic, under the leadership of General Charles de Gaulle. This brought new stability to French politics, aided by de Gaulle's own credibility and leadership, a new constitution that created a strong "semipresidential" regime, and a two-round majority voting system that helped to reinforce governmental ma-jorities (avoiding the political fragmentation and the coalition governments that resulted from the proportional representation of the Fourth Repub-lic).[5] For the first fifteen years, the Fifth Republic was characterized by a dominant Gaullist movement on the Right, supported by a small center Right "liberal" movement that was clearly overshadowed by the presi-dential machine. On the Left, the PCF remained the dominant power, maintaining its position of mutual hostility with the still anticommunist Socialists.[6] If one excludes the weak extreme Right (again overshadowed by the strong, nationalist Gaullist presence) and the weak center Right under Jean Lecanuet, France was again divided into three main parts—this time, Communists, Socialists, and Gaullists (see figure 4-1). The three parts were roughly equal in size, but the presidential system (with direct election of the president after 1962), majority voting system, and support from the center Right allowed the Gaullists to dominate. Thus the general had a relatively free hand to pursue his goals of restoring France's role as a global geopolitical actor, developing the French economy by means of state-led growth, and building a strong Europe of independent nations. During this period tariffs continued to fall within Europe, but de Gaulle put an end to the idea that economic integration would inevitably lead to the end of national sovereignty as the economic and geopolitical role of the French state grew steadily throughout the Gaullist years. Several decades later, this would make it all the more difficult for the French state, and its elites, to cope with the assault on the state implied by globalization.[7]

In the 1970s the French party system took on a new look for two reasons. The first was that the Left, finally realizing its only hope for winning power under the rules of the Fifth Republic, had united under the Common Program of the Left, which the Communists and the Socialists signed in 1972. This radical anticapitalist manifesto ended fifty years of nearly constant hostility between the two leftist movements (since the PCF broke away from Léon Blum's SFIO in 1920) and gave the Left a united platform on which to stand in the 1974 presidential election. The second important change was on the Right, which, four years after de Gaulle's death in 1970, was led (at least at the presidential level) not by the "Bonapartist" Gaullists but by the "Orléanists" under Valéry Giscard d'Estaing. Although the Gaullists still had broader support, their internal divisions and lack of leadership allowed Giscard to take over leadership of the Right. With Giscard's extremely narrow victory (425,000 votes) over François Mitterrand in the 1974 election, France was essentially divided into two parts: a Left that was anticapitalist and against the Atlantic Alliance and a Right led by the most integrationist and economically liberal leader that France had known in the postwar period. There was certainly a difference between the Left and the Right in 1974, and there were few alternatives.

Giscard had hoped to use his election to govern France from the center, arguing that the sociological changes accompanying postwar modernization and the shift from agricultural and industrial production to services and high-tech had led to a majority of potential "liberal" voters.[8] His misfortune, however, was to come to power on the eve of the 1974 oil embargo, which sent economies all over the world into a period of

Figure 4-1. *Party Share of Votes in First Ballots for National Assembly Elections, 1958–97*

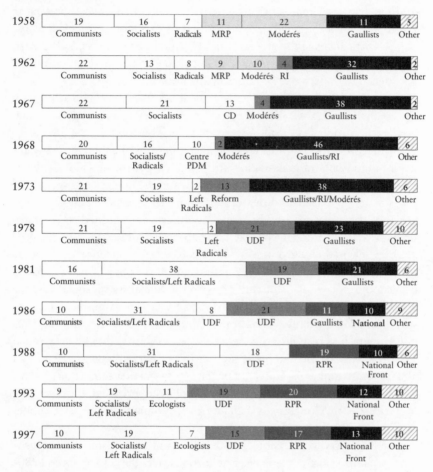

Source: Reprinted from Michael S. Lewis-Beck, ed., *How France Votes* (London: Chatham House, 2000), p. 5, copyright 2000, by permission of Chatham House Publishers.

stagflation and rising unemployment. As discussed in chapter 2, as a result of the oil shock Giscard never got a chance to implement his liberal economic program, and his efforts to do so led to the collapse of his coalition with the Gaullists on the Right. In 1976 Prime Minister Jacques Chirac resigned from the government to form a new Gaullist party, the Rassemblement pour la République (RPR). Stagflation also fueled the arguments of the anticapitalist Left, which, still united by the Common Program, looked set to win the legislative elections of 1978. But on the eve of the elections its own divisions emerged, the Common Program fell apart, and the "rightist" majority was narrowly maintained. As can be seen in figure 4-1, with the newly apparent divisions on both the Left and the Right, France was split into four almost equal parts: the PCF, the Parti Socialiste (PS), the Union pour la Démocratie Française (UDF), and the RPR, each with between 21 and 23 percent of the vote.

The Left had learned the lessons of its divisions in 1978 and would not fail again in 1981, when the seven-year presidential term—and the associated parliamentary elections—were at stake. This time the Right was divided (between its Gaullist and Orléanist wings), while the Left was once again united behind a staunchly anticapitalist platform. Taking advantage of the past seven years of slow growth and the ravages of a second oil crisis in 1979, Mitterrand denounced Giscard's allegedly passive acceptance of the consequences of global capitalism and argued for a sharp break with it. As noted in chapter 2, the program Mitterrand implemented after he defeated Giscard in May 1981 was an early rejection of the logic of globalization before the term was in vogue. If the other world economic powers did not want to pursue growth, the Socialists reasoned, France would grow its economy alone, through Keynesian stimulus. The new spending program failed disastrously, and by 1983 Mitterrand and his government had begun to pursue a new platform that looked very much like the 1976 "Barre Plan" that they had so vehemently denounced as an abdication to global capitalism. For the rest of his first term (until 1988), Mitterrand and the PS had nothing to offer but adherence to the discipline of the European Monetary System and an economic austerity plan, euphemistically labeled *rigueur*.[9]

The Socialists' conversion from extreme anticapitalism to the acceptance of Europe and a free market philosophy over the course of the 1980s is one of the most significant developments in French politics since World War II. In a manner far from the "France in three parts" of the Fourth Republic or the rigid bipolarity of the late 1970s and early 1980s, the concepts of "Left" and "Right" were now starting to lose their meaning, and new alignments were becoming possible. Indeed, the policies of the mainstream Left and Right on the most important issues—economic management, Europe, and foreign and military policy—were starting to resemble each other so much that critics began to denounce the *pensée unique* (literally, a "single way of thinking"; in this case, "the conventional wisdom") that allegedly prevailed across the political spectrum.[10] Whereas from the 1950s through the 1970s French parties were deeply divided over a wide range of issues—decolonization, cold war loyalties and alliances, economic management, nuclear and military policy, social policy, education, and European integration—many of these differences were now narrowing, leading to talk of a *république du centre*.[11] Only the fading Communists and Jean-Marie Le Pen's anti-Europe and anti-immigrant National Front stood outside the fold.

To be sure, there were differences between the rightist majority that won the 1986 parliamentary elections and the Socialist Mitterrand, with whom they "cohabited" in a divided government from 1986 to 1988. But by 1988 such differences had narrowed to the point that the presidential election between Mitterrand and Chirac seemed as much about personality as policy, with the more avuncular Mitterrand prevailing on a centrist platform. The *ouverture*—openness to cooperation with allies from the center Right—that the Socialists promised after the election never really worked out, but the fact that they proposed it showed how far France had come from the days of the rigid Left-Right split. It was now at least arguable that the Socialists and their center Right adversaries had more in common with each other, at least in policy terms, than with the growing extremes of either side.

From Europeanization to Globalization

This is the political context in which the globalization debate of the late 1990s emerged, and in which its effect on French politics must be seen. But the debate about globalization did not come out of nowhere; its clear precursor was the debate about European integration. As has already been suggested, European integration was in many ways an earlier, limited version of globalization, promising increasingly open borders to the free movement of goods, people, capital, technology, and ideas, in this case on a European rather than global level. Although easier for the French to accept than globalization, because of the more limited scale, the relative similarity of European economies, the greater commitment to social cohesion and income redistribution, the lack of a single dominant European power or culture (analogous to that of the United States in the world at large), Europeanization nonetheless challenged French society in many of the same ways. The bottom line in either case has been the need to accept influences from abroad, the rule of the market, lack of control over the domestic economy, and the declining power of the state.

All of these issues came to the fore during the divisive French debate over ratification of the Treaty on European Union (known as the Maastricht Treaty, after the Dutch city in which it was signed) during 1992. Mitterrand had originally called for a referendum for largely domestic political reasons: since opinion polls showed the French strongly in favor of European integration, Mitterrand expected to receive a show of support while weakening the Right, whose Gaullist and Orléanist wings were deeply divided over Europe. An unexpected consequence of the referendum campaign, however, was to trigger the first real public debate in France on the question of European integration. Indeed, the referendum showed that the apparent popular support for European integration resulted largely from a lack of familiarity with the real issues at stake. The majority of the French did vaguely support Europeanization, but had not really thought through the specific policy changes that it would require.[12] The Maastricht campaign thus provided the first opportunity for a public debate about the potential consequences of increasing capital movements, shifting power from states to markets, and loss of democratic control through the transfer or sharing of French sovereignty with supranational European organizations. And while the culprit for the loss of French sovereignty was not called globalization, the reasons for discontent were the same: the liberalization of trade and capital was rendering the French economy more dependent on the outside world, and therefore more vulnerable, while at the same time citizens saw their democratic prerogatives erode in favor of supranational and corporate actors. Just as in the late 1990s the World Trade Organization (WTO) would be seen as an undemocratic, foreign institution that promoted the free trade that eroded French interests and handed out rulings that supported unwelcome American exports, in the early 1990s the undemocratic bogeymen were bodies such as the European Commission and the prospective European Central Bank.

Not surprisingly, the political alignments of the debate on Europe mirrored almost exactly those that would emerge later in the decade in the debate on globalization. The opposition to European integration was led not by Left or Right, but by the margins against the center, thus putting pressure on many of the traditional alignments. On the Left, the majority of Socialists supported the government-backed treaty, which embodied their conversion to market liberalism and European integration—a long way from the Common Program of the Left. Only the iconoclastic Jean-Pierre Chevènement of the Socialists' Jacobin wing, who had already left the government in 1991 over the Gulf War, openly opposed Maastricht.

The Communists also opposed the treaty, and more generally, the *Europe des marchands* ("corporate Europe") and big capital. The Greens, newly arrived on the political scene, were deeply divided and unable to come up with an official position: Brice Lalonde, the leader of Génération Ecologie, announced that he was in favor of the treaty, but Dominique Voynet, future leader of the Green Party, opposed it.

On the Right, the great majority of the UDF joined the Socialists in campaigning for the treaty, a position consistent with their federalist aspirations and belief in the benefits of the single European market.[13] Only the "old France" branch, made up of *notables* (local barons) from the provinces, among them Philippe de Villiers, opposed the kind of Europe envisioned in the Maastricht Treaty. The internal divisions were much stronger on the Gaullist Right, however, mainly because of its insistence on the concept of sovereignty and its ambivalence about economic liberalism. The RPR, in particular, was divided over the question of Europe because the Gaullist vision of a *Europe des patries* seemed antithetical to the Europe proposed by the Maastricht Treaty. Thus RPR leader Chirac's decision to support the treaty created a split within the RPR, especially when Charles Pasqua (a traditional Gaullist and former RPR interior minister, 1986–88) and Philippe Séguin (former RPR minister for social affairs and employment, 1986–88) announced that they were voting against it. Séguin resigned from all leadership functions in the party and, along with Pasqua and de Villiers, formed the *Rassemblement pour le non au referendum* (Rally for No in the Referendum) to campaign against ratification.

In September 1992 French voters approved ratification in the referendum by a tiny majority (51 percent to 49 percent), thereby enabling the European Union to implement the Maastricht agenda. Even allowing for the fact that some of the opposition to the treaty was a protest vote against high unemployment and against a president who had by then been in power for more than 11 years, the referendum nonetheless sent a strong message of French discontent with what the great majority of their politicians were offering: more economic austerity and liberalism, enduring commitment to the *franc fort* and tight monetary policy, the erosion of French identity within the EU, and the continued—allegedly unavoidable—diminishing of national sovereignty. The same complaints would be voiced a few years later in protest not against Europe, but against the new bête noire: globalization.

Once the referendum was over and the Maastricht Treaty had come into effect (in 1993), ratified by all the other members of the EU, the

French debate over Europeanization faded significantly, and opponents of the European project were marginalized. On the Right, the main political leaders, like Chirac, had hitched their stars to the European wagon, arguing that monetary union was in France's interest, and were now not able or willing to turn back. Others who had campaigned against the treaty, like Séguin, knew how to recognize reality when they saw it, and reluctantly came to accept that continued opposition would marginalize them in French politics. As Séguin later said, "I wasn't 'for' Agincourt either, but I accept it."[14] On the Left, opposition to the EU also diminished, helped by the fact that left-of-center governments began coming to power in most of the EU countries (most important, Germany and Britain), undermining the argument that it was a liberal, free market club. Even many Communists began to see "Europe" as a possible force for social protection as much as for economic liberalization.[15]

But as "Europe" faded as the alleged cause of France's woes, it was gradually replaced by globalization. As Denis Kessler, an economist and vice president of the French employers association, the Mouvement des Entreprises Françaises (MEDEF), put it in 2000: "A few years ago, it was Europe that was being presented negatively by a large part of the French political elite: the euro was going to destroy jobs, and the loss of sovereignty would be terrible for the French economy. All of this was false. Today, we are looking for another devil—one who now has the face of globalization."[16]

It is interesting how quickly the French debate shifted, and how the anti-Europe campaign was able to morph into an even more vigorous antiglobalization movement. The change did not happen suddenly, but in several distinct steps during the course of the 1990s. Indeed, the globalization debate had been launched in 1993 (the year Maastricht came into force) with the publication of the Arthuis report on *delocalisation*.[17] Two years later, the French poured onto the streets of Paris to oppose the austerity plan of the new government led by RPR prime minister Alain Juppé. Juppé had justified this measure as a necessary step toward meeting the requirements of monetary union—that is, "Europe"—but many people also believed that it was a consequence of France's powerlessness in the face of international competition. Indeed, the 1995 strikes were seen by many on the Left as "the first great movement against globalization."[18] Two years after that, even clearer evidence that the debate about "Europe" was turning into a debate about globalization was provided by the spectacular success of Viviane Forrester's book *The Economic Horror*, which sold 350,000 copies in France in 1997.[19] Forrester, a novelist, took aim at the liberal economic thinking and practices that were spreading around the world and blamed them for nearly all of France's woes, especially unemployment and income inequality. In contrast to most of the polemics of the late 1980s and early 1990s, Forrester's main target was not Europe but global liberalism, and French people looking for alternative to the *pensée unique* rallied to her call.

It was not until 1998, however, that France's antiglobalization movement was born; the occasion of the birth was the negotiation of the Multilateral Agreement on Investment (MAI), under the auspices of the Organization for Economic Cooperation and Development (OECD). The primary objective of the MAI was to facilitate international investment by ensuring that host governments treated foreign and domestic firms similarly.[20] Negotiations had been taking place in Paris since 1997, and in spring 1998 a draft agreement was leaked to the U.S.-based consumer organization Public Citizen, which immediately denounced it as a threat to democracy, sovereignty, human rights, economic development, and the environment, and proceeded to circulate it worldwide (via the Internet, that tool of globalization). The main fear was that the MAI would limit the ability of national governments to protect their culture, environment, natural resources, and public health, and would leave their citizens vulnerable to the decisions of foreign investors, who would take only their own interests into account.

In France the first to mobilize against the MAI were nongovernmental, nonpartisan associations, such as the Association for the Taxation of Financial Transactions for the Aid of Citizens (Association pour la taxation des transactions financières pour l'aide aux citoyens, or ATTAC), Droits Devant, the Observatoire de la Mondialisation, and the Confédération Paysanne. They aggressively argued their case in the court of public opinion and garnered support from many famous personalities in the arts, including former culture minister Jack Lang, movie director Bertrand Tavernier, and actress Jeanne Moreau. Even more important, they successfully lobbied the government of Lionel Jospin, which eventually chose to pull out of the negotiations. As a result, the negotiations were halted and the multilateral initiative eventually failed. The catalytic role played by protesters in the failure of the MAI was perceived as the first major success for France's antiglobalization movement.

Antiglobalization activists, capitalizing on the success of the mobilization against the MAI, started looking for further targets. The WTO ruling in spring 1999 that the European Union's banana import regime was illegal, and therefore that the United States could implement tariffs on $193 million worth of EU exports, infuriated many in France and was fodder to the antiglobalization groups, who saw it as an unacceptable intrusion on French sovereignty in the name of protecting American corporate interests. (Although the United States is not itself a banana exporter, the leading producers of bananas in Central America are American firms, some of whose top executives have been significant donors to American political parties.) For many in France, a ruling by an unelected multinational body that the United States could punish Europe because it chose to import its bananas from poor former colonies (who seemingly had nothing else to export) was an example of corporate power and economic liberalization run amok.

The subsequent WTO ruling on hormone-treated beef in July 1999, which argued that the EU ban was protectionist, since scientific evidence did not attest to any danger to humans, further fueled these anti-American and antiglobalization sentiments. In the midst of the scare over mad cow disease and other food crises in Europe, the Geneva judges' ruling struck many in France as an example of the potential danger of loss of national control in favor of international organizations. As in the banana case, the WTO allowed the United States to retaliate against up to $116 million worth of European products of its choice. As seen in chapter 3, the fact that the resulting list of sanctioned items was disproportionately composed of French products—such as foie gras, Dijon mustard, and Roquefort cheese—helped to generate the outpouring of public support when José Bové and the Confédération Paysanne attacked the McDonald's restaurant in Millau as a symbol of all that was bad about globalization.

Another development during 1999 that provoked French debate about and opposition to globalization was the series of takeover battles among France's leading banks—Banque Nationale de Paris (BNP), Société Générale, and Paribas—discussed in chapter 2. In a country used to state-directed management of key sectors like banking, and in which hostile takeovers were rare, the French were surprised by this new brand of aggressive capitalism taking place beyond the limits of state control. The banking takeover saga was followed by another highly symbolic event in the transformation of French capitalism: in September 1999 the tire maker Michelin announced that it was laying off 7,500 employees while at the same time announcing a 17.5 percent rise in profits.[21] This extremely unpopular measure heightened the public's sense of vulnerability in the new economy and was widely denounced. It also provided antiglobalization activists with a powerful argument against the dangers of unbridled capitalism and submission to shareholders. Even the Socialist prime minister, Lionel Jospin, seemed to be announcing France's surrender to all-powerful market forces when he declared in the aftermath of the Michelin affair, "You don't regulate the economy with the law and official texts. You cannot expect the state and the government to do everything."[22]

An important step in the rise of globalization to the political forefront in France was the November 1999 WTO summit in Seattle. The meeting was intended to launch a new round of multilateral trade negotiations and—held in the home city of global exporters Microsoft, Boeing, and Starbucks—stand as a shining symbol of the successes of globalization and the free trade leadership of the United States. Already in September, however, more than a thousand French small farmers, union leaders, students, and environmental activists came together in a public meeting against globalization. The demonstrators denounced the "democraticidal" nature of the WTO and demanded a moratorium on the Seattle trade negotiations. Two months later, the antiglobalization movement managed to rally about 30,000 people in France to demonstrate against "liberal globalization" before the opening of the Seattle meeting.[23] And in Seattle itself, of course, Bové with his Roquefort was an international media star, standing as a symbol of world opposition to globalization and France's leadership of the movement. Alain Minc rightly called this the "Seattle paradox," noting that "those who protested against the omnipotence of the WTO would have been better off pushing for the reinforcement of its powers," but that was not the point.[24] The fact was that the last year of the twentieth century gave the French—and many others—sufficient reason to question the merits of a world characterized by ever more open borders, and the debate about globalization was in full force.

As the new century began, there were other signs that many in France were looking for alternatives to the program of economic liberalism and Europeanization being offered by the country's main political parties. One such sign was the steady growth of nonmainstream parties calling for alternatives to the *pensée unique*. Support for the National Front, for example, rose consistently over the 1980s and 1990s: from just 0.2 percent in the 1982 cantonal elections to 11 percent in the European elections of 1984, 14.4 percent in the presidential election of 1988, 15.1 percent in the presidential election of 1995, and 15 percent in the parliamentary election of 1997.[25] In the 1995 election, Le Pen's party got 3.8 million votes in the

Table 4-1.   *Alternance, 1978–97*

1978	Right majority in parliament reelected (Prime Minister Raymond Barre)
1981	Right president (Valéry Giscard d'Estaing) defeated by Left president (François Mitterrand)
	Right majority in National Assembly (Prime Minister Raymond Barre) replaced by Left (Prime Minister Pierre Mauroy)
1986	Left majority in National Assembly (Prime Minister Laurent Fabius) replaced by Right (Prime Minister Jacques Chirac)
1988	Right majority in National Assembly (Prime Minister Jacques Chirac) replaced by Left (Prime Minister Michel Rocard)
	Left president (Mitterrand) reelected
1993	Left majority in National Assembly (Prime Minister Pierre Bérégovoy) replaced by Right (Prime Minister Edouard Balladur)
1995	Left president (François Mitterrand) replaced by Right president (Jacques Chirac)
1997	Right majority in National Assembly (Prime Minister Alain Juppé) replaced by Left (Prime Minister Lionel Jospin)

first round, more than the UDF's 3.7 million, and 46 percent of the 8 million votes of the combined UDF-RPR—the highest such ratio in the National Front's history. The Greens, also opposed to the economic status quo and divided on Europe, gained steadily as well: from 3.8 percent in the 1995 presidential election to 7 percent in the 1997 parliamentary elections (resulting in participation in the Jospin cabinet) and 9.7 percent in the 1999 European elections. Even the Communists, now formally opposed to the Socialist Party's platform, reversed their decline. In contrast to 1986 and 1988, when the centrist parties (PS, UDF, and RPR) took 72 to 73 percent of the vote in the first round of parliamentary elections, in the 1990s the centrist scores fell to just 58 percent in both the 1993 and 1997 elections. The *pensée unique* was no longer so *unique*—except perhaps within the government itself.

Another sign of growing voter discontent during the 1980s and 1990s was the remarkable regularity of what the French call *alternance*—the replacement of the governing party with another. As shown in table 4-1, from 1978 (when the center Right majority in parliament was narrowly maintained) to 2001, every presidential and parliamentary election—with the sole exception of Chirac's election as president in 1995—resulted in a vote *against* the party in power. Even the apparent exception to the rule in 1995 was not really so, since Chirac was in effect running against his own party (and its prime minister, Edouard Balladur, was one of his opponents) on an almost leftist platform of social protection and job creation.

To be sure, several factors contributed to each election result, but the continual rejection of the party in power suggests significant discontent among French people—even if it was not clear what alternative they were hoping for.

Public and Party Opinion on Globalization

Writing in *Libération* in June 2000, public opinion specialist Jean Viard summarized the state of the French debate about globalization as follows:

> Where globalization is concerned, there are three positions. There are those who are "for" it, broadly speaking, the big shareholders. Then there are those who are "excluded" from the process, a patchwork of all those who suffer directly: the poor, workers, illegal immigrants, farmers whose markets are disappearing, etc. But most important are those in the center, the middle classes, who are on one hand fascinated by globalization and the Internet, but are afraid of losing the things that constitute their individuality: an aesthetic, a particular way of looking at culture and solidarity.[26]

While such a rough sketch is inevitably too simple, it does provide a useful framework for thinking about the breakdown of French public and party opinion on the issue. Who is in which camp, and why?

Supporters of Globalization

For all the prominence of a few media-savvy antiglobalization protesters, it is worth noting from the start that not all of the French are hostile to globalization; indeed some are highly enthusiastic about the changes that it is helping to bring to France's economic structures and its political system. Admittedly, this group is relatively small, but it is growing and could grow further as the creation of global shareholders and business leaders adds to the numbers of those who have a stake in globalization. According to French public opinion analyst Pierre Giacometti, 22 percent of the French public—whom he calls the *marchands,* or merchants, is "economically liberal" and "wants a small state, reduced to its essential functions."[27] Giacometti also identifies another group relatively open to globalization, representing 29 percent of the population, that he calls *mutants,* or mutants. Largely under thirty-five years old, *mutants* look to the future, are open to integration, and are at ease with the vocabulary and tools of the new economy—the stock market, the Internet, stock options. These figures certainly overstate the numbers of those who are "for" globalization, since it is possible to support economic globalization and the new economy while at the same time worrying about the cultural, social, or geopolitical effects. Still, it is important not to overlook the existence of proglobalization forces in France.

Some of the most prominent members of this group are iconoclastic writers and intellectuals who have been on the French scene for a long time. For instance, Guy Sorman, a professor of economics and political philosophy as well as a syndicated columnist, has written that globalization is nothing less than "the most positive thing that has happened to humanity in the twentieth century" and denounces the socialists and bureaucrats who fear its effects. Sorman thus puts Lionel Jospin and "Saint José Bové" in the same camp, the "rear guard of a movement whose very meaning has been forgotten."[28] Essayist and journalist Jean-François Revel, long a fierce opponent of communism, also supports globalization and has argued (contrary to conventional wisdom) that France in fact has a long tradition of political and economic liberalism—that predates the Gaullism and communism that have dominated the postwar period.[29] Revel is also one of the rare French thinkers to have denounced cultural protectionism. Some other commentators, mostly economists, while far less unambiguously in favor of globalization, have also written positively about it and sought to debunk many of the arguments made by the anti-globalization movement.[30]

Perhaps more important than these intellectuals, French business leaders are now getting involved in the globalization debate in a much more prominent way. Corporate executives like Jean-Marie Messier of Vivendi and Michel Bon of France Télécom represent the new image of the French business elite. They are strong proponents of the new practices of global capitalism and unabashedly take advantage of it. In his book *J6M.com*, Messier does not hesitate to praise free market capitalism, chastise "cultural exception" as a policy of isolation, and criticize the French for whom "the fans of Internet are the new barbarians."[31] Since the state has been gradually retreating from the management of the economy, and especially from the management of companies through its large-scale privatization program, one would expect the proliberalism voices to become louder and more numerous in the years to come.

Indeed, the employers movement as a whole is playing an increasingly important role in the globalization debate. The Mouvement des Entreprises de France was created in October 1997 as successor to the Conseil National du Patronat Français (CNPF), with redefined objectives and a transformed structure. Headed by industrialist Ernest-Antoine Seillière, the MEDEF vigorously seeks to promote entrepreneurship, reduce the role of the state in the management of the economy, and transform the nature of social contributions. Seillière complains that in the French way of thinking "capitalism is wrong, success is unfair, and stock options scandalous," and he spends much of his time trying to change that mentality.[32] His deputy, Denis Kessler, as noted above, is also an outspoken critic of the Socialist-led government and proponent of liberalism. While the membership of some large textile manufacturers who benefit from trade protection prevents the MEDEF from coming out unambiguously for free trade, the organization is unabashed in its support of economic liberalism and free market capitalism at a time when talking openly about these matters is still taboo across much of the French political spectrum. As Alain Minc has said, the MEDEF is "the only actor in France today to spread the liberal message in a talented and coherent way."[33] It is in this respect that the MEDEF has become a political actor in its own right, a *deuxième droite* ("second right") in the words of Isabelle Mandraud and Caroline Monnot of *Le Monde*.[34] Or as Socialist leader François Hollande has put it: "The MEDEF tends to portray itself as the first party of the opposition."[35] In the March 2001 municipal elections a number of MEDEF members even ran for office, with the strong encouragement of Seillière.[36]

The main reason why it is left to France's business elite and a few intellectuals to promote globalization and liberalization is that few French political parties are prepared to do so. Indeed, the tiny Démocratie Libérale (DL) is the only clear proponent of globalization. Formed by former industry minister Alain Madelin in 1997 as part of the UDF (and as the successor to François Léotard's Parti Républicain), DL became independent in 1998 because it wanted to promote more strongly the concepts of a federal Europe and, especially, economic liberalism. Among its proposals are to reduce the number of civil servants, decrease public spending, cut taxes, create pension funds, and set up profit-sharing programs for company workers. When Viviane Forrester published *A Strange Dictatorship* in 2000 (the sequel to *The Economic Horror* and another diatribe against the alleged evils of globalization and economic liberalism), Madelin was one of the few politicians to publicly criticize her arguments.[37] Not surprisingly, Madelin has also been highly critical of Bové, whom he believes "has got his eras, diagnosis, and remedies all wrong." Far from being a threat to France, globalization "offers a formidable opportunity to remake our society."[38]

Liberalism, Madelin argues, is not the same thing as globalization, but rather one of the answers to globalization. When the Socialist government introduced its bill on "new economic regulations," which was designed to tame the negative effects of globalization, DL led the opposition against it.[39] Madelin's policy proposals are based on the underlying premise that a free market leads to a better social and economic order than one that is distorted by state intervention. As he has noted, however, being openly liberal may be a risky strategy in French politics: "Liberalism represents a real family of thought, but it seems scary because it runs contrary to the statist tradition which defines French identity."[40] The result is the paradox that even as France increasingly adopts economic liberalism as a result of globalization, almost no one admits to being in favor of it.[41]

Critics of Globalization

Like the proponents of globalization, France's antiglobalization movement is divided into several disparate groups, both within and outside the political party system. On the Left, some of the most vocal opponents of globalization come from outside the traditional party system and have primarily channeled through associative movements. Their opposition is based mainly on social, environmental, cultural, and humanitarian concerns. On the Right, by contrast, the most successful attacks against globalization come from either the National Front or from dissident politicians who were formerly inside the traditional party system, such as Charles Pasqua and Philippe de Villiers. Their opposition is based mainly on concerns about sovereignty and the definition of national identity. But there are also many similarities between opponents of globalization on the Left and on the Right: they all want to use the power of the state to prevent the unfettered movement of people, goods, capital, and ideas from significantly changing the traditional French economy or way of life.

It is impossible to determine precisely the share of the French population that should be considered "antiglobalization," but it is probably fair to say that it is in the neighborhood of 30 to 50 percent. Using Giacometti's categorizations, this would be made up of some 18 percent from the traditional Left who "disdain money, oppose capitalism, and value equality and tolerance"—whom he calls *lutteurs,* or strugglers—plus some of the 31 percent who support a strong state and "want to protect French identity from . . . immigration, Europe, and economic change," whom he terms *gardiens,* or guardians.[42] Other polling data show that 33 percent of the French think that globalization is a "bad thing," 24 percent say that France has "more to lose" from globalization than it has to gain, and 51 percent say they agree with José Bové's views on economic and financial globalization.[43] Another general indicator might be the aggregate scores of the political parties explicitly opposed to the phenomenon in recent national elections. In the 1997 legislative elections, these included the National Front (14.9 percent), the PCF (9.9 percent), the environmentalist parties (6.2 percent), right-wing nationalists such as Philippe de Villiers's followers (6.6 percent), and Chevènement's Mouvement des Citoyens (MDC) (2 percent), for a total of 39.6 percent.[44] In the 1999 elections for the European Parliament, they included the Pasqua–de Villiers anti-Europe electoral list (13 percent); the Greens (9.7 percent); the National Front (5.7 percent); Bruno Megret's Mouvement National Républicain (MNR) (3.3 percent); Chasse, Pêche, Nature, et Tradition ("hunting, fishing, nature, and tradition") (6.8 percent); the PCF (6.8 percent); and Lutte Ouvrière/Ligue Communiste Révolutionnaire (5.2 percent), for a total of 50.5 percent.[45]

Just as is the case for the (much smaller) movement of globalization proponents, the most interesting and influential antiglobalization activists have come from outside the main political parties. Thus in 1999 it was not a politician who came to symbolize French opposition to globalization but a member of a farmers' union: José Bové. Raised partly in California but since the 1970s a sheep-farmer based in southwestern France, Bové had for several years fought in relative obscurity against the "commercialization" of the world alongside environmentalists, artists, and trade unions. It was only with his "dismantling" of McDonald's in Millau that Bové became a national and international celebrity.

Some analysts have seen in this new antiglobalization movement yet another instance of the French fear of modernity, and in Bové a reincarnation of Pierre Poujade—the small shopkeeper who united rural working-class France against economic modernization and as a result obtained 11 percent of the votes and 52 *députés* in the 1956 elections.[46] But Bové is more than a modern-day version of Poujade. The opposition to globalization presented by Bové and his followers does come in large part from a sense of vulnerability in the face of a modernizing world. And it is also to some extent a traditional protectionist movement, with groups seeking to obtain concessions from the government in defense of their interests. Yet most of the actors, including the farmers, are not pressuring their government to shelter them from international competition, but rather claim to be acting to protect the interests of the nation as a whole (if not humankind): its culture, its environment, its identity, and its sense of moral obligation. In this sense, the movement has more in common with May 1968 than with the protectionism of the 1950s. This new "global protectionism" appeals to the collective sense of identity of French society and calls for regaining some of the control that the nation has lost over its destiny. This may explain why it is so successful; and more so than if it were appealing only to one group's sense of solidarity with another.[47]

Even though they are staunchly nonpartisan and refuse to assimilate or be assimilated by existing political parties, the activists who have brought the issue of globalization to the attention of the French public are mostly from a leftist, if not extreme Left, tradition. Their heterogeneous coalition is made up of groups as diverse as ad hoc organizations, farmers, environmentalists, and trade unions.[48] Many of them, however, share a common background of humanitarian concerns, activism on behalf of developing countries, and mistrust of American capitalism.

Bové's Confédération Paysanne (CP), founded in 1987 by the fusion of several farmers' movements with roots in the 1968 revolt, seeks to promote socially and environmentally friendly agricultural policies. CP farmers have thus taken the lead in demonstrating against globalization, protesting against genetically modified crop imports, denouncing McDonald's and la malbouffe, blaming food-scares on the industrialization of agriculture, and opposing international agreements such as the MAI. In contrast to France's dominant and fiercely protectionist farming lobby, the Fédération Nationale des Syndicats d'Exploitants Agricoles (FNSEA), the CP calls for limiting public aid to 200,000 francs per farm and reducing EU agricultural exports to developing countries, so that those countries can become self-sufficient. The CP also calls for agricultural policies that preserve the rural landscape and way of life—a recognition of the "multifunctionality" of agriculture, in this case, its social rather than economic function. Also in contrast to the FNSEA, which does not hesitate to protest aggressively against imports, the CP has since 1999 focused its protests on the quality of food, both from a cultural and a public health perspective, arguing that this should be a concern of society as a whole, rather than just of a small group of industrial farmers. The campaign, as Jean-Paul Besset put it in Le Monde, was "the first time since [1968] that a farm movement has become the spokesperson of the interests of a collectivity larger than the farm itself."[49] With growing support for these positions, the CP has gradually eroded the hegemony of the FNSEA, and if it manages to establish a durable alliance with consumers, environmentalists, and other antiglobalization activists, it could have an important impact on French farming policy in the future, perhaps even making possible reform of the EU's Common Agricultural Policy (CAP).[50]

Beyond the Confédération Paysanne, the past few years have seen the creation of a number of other ad hoc antiglobalization organizations. The most well known is the Association for the Taxation of Financial Transactions for the Aid of Citizens. Created in June 1998, ATTAC claimed more than 34,000 members as of May 2001—and the sympathies of an impressive 130 members of the French parliament.[51] (By way of comparison, the Green Party, which is part of the government, had just 6,000 members.) The association was created in the wake of an influential editorial entitled "Disarm the markets" by Ignacio Ramonet, editor of the radical monthly *Le Monde Diplomatique*.[52] Ramonet had called for a worldwide tax on financial transactions, referred to as the Tobin tax after Nobel Prize–winning economist James Tobin, who first put the idea forward in 1971. The idea is that the tax on short-term financial transactions would deter speculation (since shifting funds back and forth would ultimately become very expensive), and the revenue could be used to compensate those "punished" by globalization. Presided over by Bernard Cassen, director general of *Le Monde Diplomatique*, and managed by Pierre Tartakowsky, editor of *Options* (a trade union magazine), ATTAC is targeted toward the middle class and seeks to become the uncontested antiglobalization lobby. Numerous academics also support ATTAC, leading economist Bernard Maris to observe that it is the first time since 1968 that academics have left their ivory tower to take an active part in the social debate.[53] *Le Monde Diplomatique* is a key tool in the success of ATTAC, with a circulation of 300,000—and an estimated 900,000 readers—in France alone.[54]

Another active ad hoc organization is the Observatoire de la Mondialisation, led by an American expatriate, Susan George. Created in 1997 as a French spinoff of the American International Forum on Globalization, it is composed mainly of academics and intellectuals. Its goal is to become an activist think tank with influence over French and international politics.[55] It achieved its first victory in 1998 with its testimony to the commission on the MAI headed by Catherine Lalumière, who was among those who helped to persuade the Jospin government to withdraw its support for the agreement. The Observatoire also played an important role in mobilizing and coordinating French NGO participation in the WTO meeting in Seattle in November 1999. It subsequently proved an actor with some political influence during the French presidency of the European Union, in the second half of 2000, when it again mobilized a campaign against the proposed revision of the EU rules for trade policymaking.[56]

Finally, among the very diverse coalition of nonpartisan antiglobalization activists are those outside the mainstream trade union and associative movements. Most prominent among these is Droits Devant!, an association created in 1994 to defend the *"sans"* ("-less"): *sans-papiers* (illegal immigrants), *sans-logement* (homeless), and *sans-travail* (jobless). It is headed by Jean-Claude Amara and Pierre Contesenne, of the trade union SUD-Aérien, both of whom come from the tradition of "anarcho-syndicalism."[57] Trade unions such as SUD and the Groupe des Dix, many of them born from the December 1995 strike, have also joined in the antiglobalization fight. The Coordination pour le Contrôle Citoyen de l'OMC (CCC-OMC, that is, the Coordination for Citizens' Oversight of the WTO), created in 1998, groups about 95 of these diverse associations, trade unions, and so-called new social movements.

The antiglobalization debate is thus dominated by groups outside the traditional party structure, but some parties, both from the Left and from the Right, also feature strong antiglobalization messages in their platforms. On the Left, the Mouvement des Citoyens, led by Jean-Pierre Chevènement, has developed the *"souverainiste"* message, a combination of fear for national sovereignty, centrality of the state, and the democratic deficit.[58] The MDC was founded in 1992 when Chevènement pulled his "Socialisme et République" faction (formerly the Centre d'Etudes, Recherches, et d'Education Socialiste, or CERES) out of the Socialist Party, having resigned as Defense Minister during the 1990–91 Gulf War. The MDC opposes the U.S.-led world order that has emerged from the fall of the Soviet Union, and the "liberal" Europe sanctioned by the Maastricht Treaty. It calls for a definition of Europe that includes Russia but not the United States.[59] Some prominent members of the Socialist Party—such as Julien Dray, Henri Emmanuelli, Jean-Christophe Cambadélis, and Harlem Désir—have also publicly expressed their support for the antiglobalization movement.[60]

The Communist Party also officially denounces globalization. This is the logical extension of its struggle against capitalism. To some extent, the new globalization debate has given the Communists a new *raison d'être* after a period—from the early 1980s to the mid-1990s—in which their share of the national vote fell by more than 50 percent. Indeed, long-standing anticommunist Jean-François Revel argues that the fight against globalization has replaced the now defeated fight against capitalism as the new ideology of the far Left: "The intensification of the verbal and ideological struggle [against globalization] comes precisely from the disappearance of communism. . . . Now that communism has disappeared, it has become again a pure utopia, therefore perfect."[61] In October 1999 the PCF organized an antiglobalization demonstration that drew more than 50,000 participants, and in March 2000 it made the struggle against globalization a major theme of its thirtieth congress.[62] For PCF leader Robert Hue, the 1999 WTO meeting in Seattle was "a reflection of a capitalist and ultraliberal globalization gone wild. We've got to get hold of it, the people must be heard."[63] Not surprisingly, 71 percent of Communist Party voters see globalization as a threat to French jobs and companies, compared with only 20 percent who see it as an opportunity.[64]

The Greens have also tried to get political mileage out of globalization, which they argue is responsible for the industrialization of agriculture, genetically modified organisms, and global health scares such as mad cow disease. They vow to fight to preserve the environment against the evils of globalization. They also blame "the widespread computerization of the work process, the globalization of commerce, and economic liberalism" for unemployment.[65]

On the Right, the opposition to globalization has come first and foremost from the National Front, which recently has been joined by defectors from the more mainstream Right. Building on his attacks on European integration, Jean-Marie Le Pen now denounces globalization as the "enemy number one" of France. "It is evident that globalization and its Trojan horse, federal Europe, are pushing for the death of France," he argued at a National Front conference in April 2000.[66] Opposition to globalization is the logical extension of the National Front's fight against foreign influences. The National Front has long perpetuated the republican revolutionary legend of a homogeneous nation, where "integration" (assimilation) is the keyword, and therefore "national preference" a guiding principle for policy. The appeal of Le Pen's message comes primarily from his linkage of domestic economic insecurities to external threats. Initially, his central claim was that France's high unemployment was the result of the "invasion" of immigrants, which in turn threatened national identity. The growing popularity of this message throughout the 1980s led to the adoption of the theme of a threatened national identity in mainstream political discourse. In large part, the debate on France and its borders initiated by the National Front prepared the way for the debate on Europe in the early 1990s.

The National Front continues to portray Europeanization and liberal market forces as direct attacks on French national identity. Having initially denounced immigration and the free flow of goods, labor, and capital as the main causes of France's economic woes, the FN gradually shifted its focus to European integration, and then to globalization. Indeed, Le Pen chose trade globalization instead of immigration as the central theme of his electoral campaign for the June 1999 elections to the European Parliament. But Le Pen has not been able to capitalize politically on either underlying popular feelings about immigration or the centrality of the debate on globalization.

The year 1999 saw the implosion of the National Front. That year, Bruno Megret and his supporters broke ranks with the FN to create their own far Right party, the Mouvement National Républicain. Personal animosity, more than ideological divisions, differentiates the two parties. Megret has adopted the old FN discourse, with its focus on immigration. Meanwhile, Le Pen has at least made the pretense of seeking to bring the FN closer to the center, including a "beur" (second-generation French citizen of North African descent) in its political committee and playing down the theme of immigration, replacing it instead with a crusade against globalization and the "communist threat." Neither strategy has proved successful.

During the 1999 European elections, Le Pen's National Front won 5.7 percent of the votes, while Megret's MNR obtained only 3.3 percent. These results were considered a defeat for both far Right movements, compared with the scores obtained by the National Front in previous elections in the 1990s. Since the European elections, Le Pen and Megret's constant attacks against each other have only served to further damage the far Right.[67] Moreover, Le Pen himself has become ineligible for office following a violent altercation with a Socialist candidate in local elections in 1997.

Another party on the Right, however, has taken up this antiglobalization discourse to its advantage. The alliance between Philippe de Villiers, formerly of the UDF, and Charles Pasqua, formerly of the RPR, for the European elections in June 1999 ran on an anti-European, antiglobalization platform and won 13 percent of the votes—more than the RPR. This success led to the official founding of the Rassemblement pour la France (RPF, recalling de Gaulle's party of the same name) in November 1999, whose charter focuses on the sovereignty of the French nation, the alliance of economic freedom and social cohesion in order to resist globalization, and the centrality of French values. The party was built around the *souverainiste* idea that French leaders have given up in the face of globalization and the race for money everything that made France a great nation.[68] Contrary to the general abdication of successive French governments to the forces of globalization, multinational companies and supranational institutions, the RPF founders argued that France should regain control of its destiny and "take charge." Pasqua could not have been clearer about his opposition to globalization, "this new totalitarianism of our time that presents itself under this welcoming name of 'globalization,' whereas in reality it is nothing but the subjugation of people, languages, and nations to the commercial interests of multinational groups and the hegemonic global will of the United States."[69]

But the *souverainiste* movement subsequently suffered a setback, as fundamental misunderstandings and personal rivalry between its two leaders led to the implosion of the party in July 2000. Villiers, a representative of the Catholic conservative Right, wanted to create a genuine *souverainiste* party of the Right. Pasqua, on the other hand, representing the populist, Bonapartist Right, wanted to attract all *souverainistes*, from the Right and the Left. The RPF may not survive the split between its leaders, but its demise in 2000 was attributable more to personal conflict than to the rejection of its ideas. As the results of the Maastricht referendum and the initial support gathered by the RPF suggest, there is ample room on the Right for a *souverainiste* challenge to the traditional parties.

The Centrist Majority

The majority of French people—and their political representatives—are neither unambiguously enthusiastic about nor unremittingly hostile to globalization. They are somewhere in between, in the sense that most seem to recognize the power of globalization to create wealth, but worry at the same time that it threatens both the French social model and French culture and identity. This ambiguity emerges clearly from opinion polls: While 53 percent of the French think that globalization is "a good thing for France" (as against 35 percent who say it is "bad for France") and 58 percent say that France has more to gain from globalization (compared with 24 percent who say it has "more to lose"), 72 percent are "suspicious" of globalization (compared with 24 percent who are "confident"). Similarly, whereas 59 percent believe that globalization will "make firms more competitive," 63 percent believe that it is "good for the rich and a danger to the poor"; 59 percent believe that it will be good for companies

(25 percent disagree), but only 36 percent believe it will be good for workers (46 percent disagree).[70] It is impossible to know exactly how many of the French fit into this category of "fascinated but afraid," but it probably includes most of Giacometti's *mutants, gardiens,* and *marchands,* leaving only the irredeemably hostile *lutteurs.*

The ambiguity of the majority of the public is reflected in the positions of the mainstream political parties—most of the PS, the UDF, and the RPR. Indeed the attitude toward globalization of each of these parties and their main representatives can best be summed up as "yes, but": yes to globalization, but only if it is controlled and managed in a way that protects French culture, identity, and society. While there are obvious differences among the main parties on particular issues related to how the country is adapting to globalization—the Socialists, for example, are more skeptical of economic liberalism than much of the center Right, and the Gaullists take a tougher line than the Left on defending the French language—the differences are relatively narrow, and are often more rhetorical than substantive. The factions of the mainstream parties that cannot live within this general consensus on globalization—the MDC on the Left and DL and the RPF on the Right—have now broken off, leaving the "central group" to adopt broadly similar positions on the need to accept but manage globalization. Whereas as recently as the early 1980s the French Left was seeking to "break with capitalism," and in 1986–88 the Right briefly flirted with neoliberalism, today the main French parties find themselves on similar ground in the major economic debates.

For the Socialists, it is Prime Minister Jospin who has taken the lead in trying to define his party's approach to globalization. He describes it as a phenomenon that presents both opportunities and risks: "Globalization is not a single movement. If it unifies, it also divides. If it creates formidable progress, it risks creating or prolonging unacceptable inequalities. While it opens up cultures to one another, it threatens homogenization and uniformity. If it liberates energies, it also stimulates negative forces that must be tamed."[71]

To deal with these contradictory tendencies, Jospin calls for an approach that blends traditional socialism—including an interventionist, activist state—with the free market. And while he has gone out of his way to distinguish himself from the so-called Third Way movement led by Bill Clinton, Tony Blair, and Gerhard Schroeder, his socialism is nonetheless tinged with pragmatism, both in its rhetoric and in its policy. Jospin defined his approach to "modern socialism" in a pamphlet written for the Fabian Society:

> Social democracy is a way of regulating society and of putting the market economy at the service of the people. . . . On this basis we accept the market economy, because it is the most effective means—provided it is regulated and managed—of allocating resources, stimulating initiative, and rewarding effort and work. But we reject "the market society." For although the market produces wealth in itself, it generates neither solidarity nor values, neither objectives nor meaning. Because society is far more than an exchange of goods, the market cannot be its only driving force.[72]

As noted above, the Socialist Party (let alone Jospin's coalition government) is diverse, ranging from the Socialist members of parliament who are in the forefront of the fight against globalization to those with a much more centrist way of thinking, like the former and current finance ministers, Dominique Strauss-Kahn and Laurent Fabius. But in the party as a whole—and the government it is a part of—Jospin has had little trouble imposing his pragmatic policies accompanied by more ideological rhetoric. Arguably, even ostensibly *dirigiste* measures like the flagship thiry-five-hour work week (put forward as a campaign slogan in an election that the Left did not expect to win), were designed in part to protect the government's Left flank while it proceeded with much more liberal policies like privatization, tax cuts, and stock options.

How the French government is attempting to manage and regulate globalization is the subject of the concluding chapter of this book. Here, we note simply the degree of convergence on these issues between the center Left and the center Right. Indeed, Chirac's statements on globalization and how to approach it are difficult to distinguish from Jospin's—both agree that it can have positive effects but also stress that it can threaten identities and undermine social equality and that it must be controlled by regulation. As Chirac stated in his July 14, 2000, address to the nation, "Globalization is, by definition, a great force of progress, in that it can accelerate interaction and trade, which is now how wealth is best created. But it also involves serious dangers. If we're not careful, it will considerably accentuate the phenomenon of exclusion. . . . [Globalization] can only be tamed by an international agreement. Making a profit is entirely legitimate, but that doesn't mean you can do just anything."[73] The themes of Chirac's long article in *Le Figaro,* "Humaniser la mondialisation," are almost exactly the same as those of Jospin's long article, "Maîtriser la mondialisation," published in *Les Echos* three months previously.[74]

Chirac has almost entirely abandoned the neoliberalism he espoused in 1986–88, and indeed he was elected president in 1995 on a campaign platform that could well have been that of a Socialist candidate: emphasising the need to address unemployment, reduce inequalities, and use the state to support the socially and economically "excluded."[75] Later that year, the Juppé government did attempt to reduce some social benefits as part of its plan to shore up the social security system and prepare for European monetary union, but Juppé was forced to resign in the face of public protests, and Chirac went back to his "social" rhetoric.[76]

With a left-wing coalition in power since 1997, one might have expected Chirac and the rest of the center Right to adopt a liberal course in opposition, as they did in 1986–88, but they have not. Indeed, this is one reason why Alain Madelin, the neoliberal former minister of the economy felt the need to break out on his own to create Démocratie Libérale, and why the MEDEF has felt it necessary to become more politically active. Other center Right leaders, like François Bayrou, talk about the need to "moralize the market" and "associate it with international solidarity."[77] Bayrou has even come out in favor of the Tobin tax. And in a manner not so different from that of Jospin and the center Left, Pierre Méhaignerie (UDF-FD) also seeks to strike a balance between "adapting to globalization" and "making sure that competition rules are respected and that takeovers do not have serious social consequences."[78] To be sure, there are differences between Left and Right over the French response to globalization—the thirty-five-hour work week is probably the best example. What is true, and striking, however, is that these differences are far less significant than those that divide the PS from the rest of the Left and the RPR-UDF from the rest of the Right. This has perhaps been globalization's greatest domestic political effect.

Conclusion

Several conclusions can be drawn from this discussion of globalization's impact on French domestic politics. First, it is clear that for all the prominence of José Bové and other critics, the majority of the French are not deeply hostile to globalization. Rather, most are ambivalent; they see the advantages and worry about the effects. But it is also clear that the antiglobalization movement is strong enough, and the ambivalence of the majority pronounced enough, that even mainstream political leaders must take antiglobalization sentiment into account. This is clear from the policies, or at least the rhetoric, of political leaders on both the Left and the Right—Jospin's rejection of the "dictatorship of the shareholders" and Chirac's refusal to submit to the will of "pensioners in California."[79] Even as they liberalize the economy and recognize the ongoing reduction in state control, French policymakers must continue to talk as if they are in control.

One example of the impact of the antiglobalization movement is how the government has treated the Bové phenomenon. Far from ostracizing Bové as a dangerous radical with whom he had nothing in common, Jospin has described Bové as a "vigorous and strong personality . . . who reflects the French people's traditional radicalism."[80] The prime minister even took Bové to dinner and pointed out, for good measure, that he had never been a big fan of McDonald's himself ("Je ne suis pas personnellement très McDo").[81] After the Left's poor showing in the March 2001 municipal elections, Jospin again reached out to the antiglobalization movement, his chief of staff going so far as to seek to hire an "antiglobalization adviser" for the prime minister's office.[82] Chirac has also expressed his "complete solidarity" with French farm workers, announced that he "detests" McDonald's, and made a point of showing more sympathy than opposition to José Bové.[83] After the large and violent antiglobalization protests at the G-8 summit in Genoa, Italy, in July 2001, both Chirac and Jospin distinguished themselves from other G-8 leaders by stressing the need to "understand" the feelings of the protesters.[84]

The history of the debate over the Tobin tax is another good illustration of the mainstream parties' need to take account of the public's unease with globalization. Initially, Finance Minister Laurent Fabius strongly opposed the principle of the Tobin tax, which has been the pet project of the antiglobalization movement. Faced with the strength of that movement (and the fact that 130 members of parliament are members of ATTAC), however, Fabius eventually changed his stance. In late June 2000, not coincidentally as Bové's trial was under way in front of the watchful eyes of tens of thousands of supporters, Fabius indicated that he was sympathetic to the Tobin tax.[85] Jospin, who had initially supported the Tobin tax during his presidential election campaign in 1995 but abandoned it as unrealistic in 1998, underwent a similar conversion at around the same time. On July 1, 2000, he declared that he, too, would "think again" about the Tobin tax.[86] By April 2001, perhaps not unrelated to the Left's poor results in the municipal elections the previous month, Jospin was calling on the International Monetary Fund to reconsider whether the Tobin tax could be implemented after all.[87] As already argued, none of this is to say that there is no difference between the government and the antiglobalization Left, but the former cannot ignore the latter.

That French leaders took so seriously the first "social world forum" in Porto Alegre, Brazil, in January 2001 is another illustration of the importance of antiglobalization rhetoric in France today. Although more senior officials represented France at the 2001 World Economic Forum in Davos, Switzerland, it is nonetheless significant that Jospin felt obliged to send two ministers, including Trade Minister François Huwart, to the "counter-Davos" summit in Porto Alegre, where they joined antiglobalization figures like Bové, Chevènement, and Alain Krivine—leader of the far Left Ligue Communiste Révolutionnaire.[88]

Perhaps most striking of all has been the government's reaction to economic developments such as the job reductions announced by Michelin in September 1999 and the decisions by Marks & Spencer and Danone to close stores and factories in France in March 2001. Far from seeking to explain to the public that closing unprofitable branches was the best way for a company to remain competitive, and thereby preserve the tens of thousands of other jobs that depend on this competitiveness, the government and many prominent politicians joined the denunciations of these companies, some even supporting calls to boycott Danone's products unless it reversed its decision.[89] Clearly, even as the French adapt to and benefit from economic globalization, they are not prepared to accept all its consequences without resistance, and their governments are not prepared to run the risk of trying to lead or persuade public opinion to the contrary.

A related conclusion is that the labels "Left" and "Right" are becoming less and less accurate. On issues that involve globalization, the mainstream parties certainly have more in common with their counterparts on the other side of the Left-Right divide than with the extremes on the same side of the political spectrum. As this chapter has shown, the Socialist government and the moderate Right opposition have fundamentally similar visions of the advantages and dangers of globalization. The same is true for the outright opponents of globalization. One would not often expect natural agreement between a hard-line rightist former interior minister and a left-wing rebel, but while Charles Pasqua and José Bové have little else in common, on many aspects of globalization they stand together. At the time of his trial for vandalizing a McDonald's restaurant in June 2000, Pasqua wished Bové good luck, called his "battle" legitimate, and thanked him for having helped ruin the Seattle WTO negotiations.[90] The normalization of *cohabitation,* now in its third incarnation since the mid-1980s, may be evidence of this ideological convergence between the center Left and the center Right.[91]

The basic party structure of the Fifth Republic has, of course, remained in place and is unlikely to disintegrate any time soon, since other fundamental historical cleavages still separate the Left from the Right. But the debate over globalization strains each side and makes it difficult for each side to unite. At present the main threat of fragmentation seems to be on the Right, which has proven unable to react in a unified fashion to recent political and economic challenges. The emergence of small parties (such as the RPF and DL), the disarray of the RPR, and the implosion of the National Front are all testimony to the difficulties faced by the French right today. But similarly, the adoption of liberal economic policies by the Socialist government could open the way for a leftist challenge—particularly if the economic recovery were to stall, and unemployment started to rise once more. The resurrection of "Left of Left" activist movements, the relative success of the Greens, and the stabilization of support for the PCF after decades of decline are all indicators that the unity of the Left is not forever guaranteed either.

A further conclusion is that the French are revising their expectations about politics as globalization reveals the powerlessness of politicians to deal with broad economic phenomena. This is one of the lessons that can be drawn from the results of the March 2001 municipal elections. On the one hand, these elections were a clear defeat for the government (except in the big cities of Paris and Lyon), signaling public discontent with current policies even in economic prosperity. On the other hand, these elections can also be read as a sign that French politics is becoming more local, like American politics.[92] Many of the successful candidates focused on local issues such as roads, security, and public parks. If politicians can no longer do anything about the big picture because of the forces of globalization, so the reasoning goes, at least they can make a difference closer to home.

Finally, globalization is helping to change some fundamental aspects of French political culture that have been in place for decades, if not longer. The political process has long been heavily dominated by the state and by political parties. But these features of French politics are changing.

Privatization, liberalization, and freer trade have created a new breed of capitalists who no longer rely on the state for guidance. Along with strong growth, they have also empowered a new generation of young entrepreneurs, more often trained at an Anglo-Saxon-style business school than at the Ecole Nationale d'Administration (ENA), as would have been the case in the past.[93] More than ever before, business leaders individually, and a very vocal MEDEF collectively, are speaking up and playing a political role.

In the antiglobalization camp, outside actors have also begun to play an important role in the political debate. These include groups like Bové's Confédération Paysanne, which has begun to impose its views about agriculture and free trade on the rest of the agricultural unions; ATTAC, which has used its popular support and 130 members in parliament to influence the French debate about international finance; and the Observatoire de la Mondialisation, which can claim credit for having helped to end the MAI negotiations. Ironically, these antiglobalization groups are now benefiting greatly from increased contact with activists in other countries, which has given them both ammunition for their struggle (through arguments and mobilization) and legitimacy (through emulation). NGOs had never been very prominent in statist France, but they will now have to be taken into account.

CHAPTER FIVE

The French Response: Managing Globalization

> "The more the world globalizes, the more it needs rules."
> *Lionel Jospin, speech to the UN General Assembly,*
> *September 20, 1999*

> "Globalization can only be managed by international agreement."
> *Jacques Chirac, speech to the nation, July 14, 2000*

As France enters the twenty-first century, globalization is one of its greatest challenges. While the technological advances, economic freedoms, and social and cultural opportunities that accompany it clearly bring major benefits to most French people, globalization also threatens to undermine some fundamental features of French society—the tradition of state-centered capitalism, in which citizens count on the state rather than the market to ensure their welfare; certain aspects of French culture and identity, including language, food, art, and traditional way of life; the republican tradition emphasizing equality and fraternity over efficiency; and the enduring desire to play an influential global role. It is no wonder that many of the French are at best ambivalent about, and in some cases downright hostile to, the phenomenon.

As previous chapters have shown, French opposition to globalization is not uniform, despite the impression given by the country's activist—and now famous—antiglobalization movement. Indeed, one of the most interesting conclusions to emerge from this study is the gap between the widespread perception that France has barely adapted to globalization, particularly in the economic area, and the reality that it has actually adapted to a considerable degree. As chapter 2 in particular showed, the French economy has been dramatically transformed over the past two decades, a transformation that is now finally paying off in terms of economic performance in practically every measurable category. No one can look at the extent of France's integration in the world economy today—in terms of foreign direct investment, global corporate mergers, international trade, stock markets, stock options, technology, and the Internet—and conclude that the country has not dramatically "globalized" in a way that was almost unimaginable just twenty years ago.

The truth about French attitudes toward globalization is that most of the French are apprehensive about globalization, but not necessarily opposed to it. Most French people fall somewhere between the two extremes of opinion represented by José Bové with his Roquefort and Jean-Marie Messier with his multinational, high-tech conglomerate. In fact as chapter 4 argues, the majority of the French people and their political representatives fall into the category of "fascinated but afraid." They share the basic view that globalization is inevitable and largely beneficial to France, but they are also convinced that it must be contained, tamed, shaped, and managed to curb its most damaging effects. The French call this *mondialisation maîtrisée*—perhaps best translated as "managed" globalization. This is the French response to the challenge of globalization.

To a certain degree, the notion of *mondialisation maîtrisée* is political rhetoric—the sort of language one would expect political leaders to use in a country where people look to the state to protect them from the vagaries of national and international life. Indeed, as a member of Lionel Jospin's government candidly told one of the authors of this book, "France has a culture of *volontarisme* [reliance on a strong state]. French leaders cannot just sit back and tell people there is nothing they can do. The people look to them for proposals, ideas, and initiatives. This is not to say that French ideas on managing globalization are solely for the purpose of giving people the impression that the state is still in charge, but there is no doubt that this is part of it."[1] The Jospin government, in particular, has been adept at masking the degree to which France is adapting to a globalized world through the use of reassuring rhetoric about regulating capitalism, highly symbolic efforts to control the free market (such as the introduction of the thirty-five-hour work week and the "new economic regulations"), and the pursuit of cultural and trade policies designed to protect the French identity that many feel is under threat.

Mondialisation maîtrisée, however, is not merely rhetorical. It is bolstered and given meaning by a set of domestic and international policies designed not just to shield the French state government from criticism, but actually to shield the French people, and others around the world, from globalization's negative effects. Just as the French have had their own model is so many domains—planned capitalism after the war, a special role in the Atlantic Alliance, privatization through *noyaux durs* ("hard cores" of trusted investors)—the French response to globalization is also distinctive. It can be seen at work in five areas: domestic policies to preserve the state; a commitment to Europe; trade policies to protect workers' rights, the environment, and food safety; proposals for international financial reform; and efforts to preserve France's international diplomatic and strategic role.

Preserving the State

France's *dirigiste* model—in which the state is the dominant actor in society—is under direct assault from globalization. Whereas under *dirigisme* the state owns much of the national means of production, directly employs large number of workers, and taxes heavily to promote redistribution, as a result of globalization the state loses control and the market takes over. Privatized firms act according to their balance sheets and shareholder interests rather than under national direction; the stock market dictates economic decisions more often than the government; and new forces in society, from civic action groups to business executives, play a greater role than bureaucrats, officials, and political parties. All of these things are happening in France today, putting under strain a social and economic model that served France well in the postwar period and to which many French people remain closely attached.

While very real, however, the withering of the French state should not be exaggerated, and French leaders of both the Left and the Right are determined to see that it not go too far. As pointed out in chapter 2, government spending as a share of GDP has stopped rising, but it is still above 50 percent and among the highest in the world—hardly a sign of a "minimal state." Similarly, French spending on the welfare state is over 30 percent of GDP, third highest in the world, after Sweden and Denmark—again, hardly an example of the abdication of French citizens' welfare to the global market.[2] Health care spending, more than 75 percent of which comes from the state, consumes nearly 10 percent of French GDP, giving France what the World Health Organization has called the most effective health care system in the world.[3] The state is responsible for running and financing the expensive French pension system, and Jospin has made clear (in the face of public resistance) that he has no intention of changing this.[4] Even if the Right were to win a strong majority in the next parliament, one would expect significant resistance to a further reduction in the state's role in France's economy and society.

As we have shown, the Jospin government has played an important role in continuing to convince the French Socialist party of the need to accept the global market, but Jospin has also made it clear that he does not believe that the state is impotent in the face of the changes wrought by globalization. "We cannot let supposedly natural economic laws guide the evolution of our societies," he insists. "This would be an abdication of our political responsibilities. On the contrary, we must seek to govern the forces that are at work in economic globalization."[5] He argues that the "need to take control in adapting to reality places a special responsibility on the state. The state is in a position to provide the necessary direction without taking the place of other actors in society."[6]

Jospin's flagship economic program, the thirty-five-hour work week, coupled with a major state-run jobs program for the young and long-term unemployed, provides a classic example of how his government is seeking to use the power of the *volontariste* state to cushion the negative effects of globalization—and it is highly popular with the French.[7] These programs contravene the demands of global liberalism and unimpeded international competition and emphasize quality of life and equality over productivity and income generation. The government has also made clear that even if it is moving ahead with privatization in ways that few would have thought possible even five years ago, there are limits to the process: the French seem unlikely to back away from the notion that it is the state's duty to provide access to public services like transportation, energy, and health care to all, which in most cases means maintaining a direct role for the state.

The Right, while critical of what it calls Jospin's leftist views (and in particular, the thirty-five-hour work week), does not have a fundamentally different approach. When it did try to slightly reduce state provision of jobs and pensions in late 1995 (after Jacques Chirac had become president by running a left-wing campaign), protests in the streets forced the government to back down and helped contribute to its electoral defeat in 1997. Indeed it seems quite clear that the French people, even as they increasingly accept the market as the main basis for their economy, continue to want a strong state. Most grudgingly accept that the days of government jobs and generous handouts are disappearing, but they continue to resist the process. Even as they adapt to globalization (or perhaps because they are doing so), the French seem to be asking for *more* state, rather than less. According to a poll taken in September 1999, 53 percent of the French said the state did not intervene enough in the economy, compared with only 17 percent who said it intervened too much. Likewise, when asked about employment (80 percent responded "not enough" state intervention, compared with 6 percent saying there was "too much"), the environment (68 percent and 7 percent, respectively), health care (61 and 10 percent), transportation (59 percent and 9 percent), food security (58 percent and 6 percent), and business activity (45 percent and 21 percent), public opinion was overwhelmingly favorable toward state intervention.[8] In short, the French are looking for their own way of adapting to globalization, but that only means making adjustments to the role of the state, not its abdication.

Building a Strong Europe

Another key element in the French response to globalization—at least, that of the government and the main political parties—is Europe. Even as they make clear their unwillingness to allow the state to abandon its role of protecting its citizens, French leaders are increasingly convinced that their best hope of maintaining some control is through the European Union. As President Chirac put it on the eve of France's EU presidency in June 2000, "there is no alternative to the construction of Europe if we want . . . to preserve and defend our values against the challenge of globalization."[9] Jospin echoed the thought in his major speech on Europe in May 2000, saying that Europe's "vocation" was "to orient globalization toward the rule of law and justice."[10] French leaders recognize that in an increasingly integrated world, Europeans acting together can play a much more influential role than can France acting alone.

The EU is seen as a tool to help manage the effects of globalization in a number of ways. By providing a large single market, the EU allows France and other member states to take advantage of many of the benefits of globalization (comparative advantage; free circulation of goods, services, money, and people) on a more limited scale and among relatively like-minded countries at similar levels of economic development. France finds it easier to accept European integration than global integration because of the Europeans' similar value systems and common commitment to generous social and environmental provisions—what Jospin calls "a model of regulation that puts man at the heart of globalization."[11] The French EU trade commissioner, Pascal Lamy, has also argued that whereas many see Europe as "just an instrument for advancing globalization," it is "in fact the only instrument for harnessing the forces of globalization to make it compatible with our model of society." To do this, Lamy calls for "necessary regulation in the economic, social, and environmental fields; a balance between competition and cooperation; and the necessary institutional arrangements to allow for the development, adoption, implementation, and enforcement of rules."[12]

A Europe united around the idea that globalization must be "mastered" can also wield much more influence in international negotiations, whether they be on trade, the environment, food safety, international financial reform, foreign policy, the cultural exception, or anything else. France alone arguably could never successfully stand up to the Americans in any of these areas, but the EU—with GDP and population on a par with or even greater than those of the United States—has increasingly done so.[13] The United States' willingness to offer amendments to its foreign sales corporation tax scheme (an arrangement that allows U.S. companies to lower their taxes by using shell companies based outside the United States) and its agreement not to implement secondary sanctions on European companies that are part of the Libertad Act (Cuba) and Iran-Libya Sanctions Act are two recent examples that show how Europe's trade leverage can win concessions.[14] Indeed, Europe's ability to act as a unit on trade questions was one of the factors that led the United States to agree to the creation of a World Trade Organization with a binding dispute mechanism.

The creation of the euro has also provided protection from the vicissitudes of globalization, sheltering more than half of the trade of participating EU countries from international currency fluctuations. Furthermore, if the euro proves to be a success, it may one day allow Europeans to invoice energy imports in their own currency (instead of in dollars) and become a reserve currency rivaling the dollar.[15] The French have called for a reinforcement of the Eurogroup, the twelve countries participating in the single currency, to help it play a greater international role.

Finally, as we discuss below, Europe's growing and increasingly successful efforts to formulate a common foreign and security policy—and to develop the political and military means to implement it—also help EU members to control their fate in a globalizing world that otherwise tends to favor the United States. For all these reasons, Europe is a relatively consensual issue in French politics and public opinion, with the exception of the extremist parties and the *souverainistes*. Even the PCF now sees Europe more as a means to protect the French from global capitalism than as a tool to promote it, and José Bové believes that Europe "can be a motor" in promoting the notion that markets must be controlled.[16]

While the mainstream parties hold strongly to the view that Europe is a shield against the worst effects of globalization, the French public seems more divided on this point. Indeed, when polled in mid-2001 about the relationship between European integration and globalization, 40 percent of respondants believed the EU constituted a means to protect France against the effects of globalization, compared with 54 percent who believed that Europe reinforced globalization's effects.[17] (The poll did not, however, ask whether the effects seen to have been reinforced were positive or negative.) On a more general level, there seems to be widespread French support for European integration. As figure 5-1 shows, after falling steadily from a peak of over 74 percent in 1987, the proportion of French people who believed that EU membership was a "good thing" for France stabilized in the late 1990s at around 49 percent (with just 14 percent saying it was a "bad thing"); and the proportion of those who felt that France "benefits from EU membership" rose from its 1993 low point of 40 percent after the Maastricht referendum to 49 percent in 2000. With a slight qualification—"*rather* a good thing" (*plutôt une bonne chose*)— the level of support for EU membership rises to 80 percent.[18] It is also worth noting that a far greater percentage of people in France want the pace of European integration to increase (51 percent) than want it to decrease (9 percent).[19]

This does not necessarily mean that there is support for a federalist, supranational Europe: polls show that while a slim majority of the French (53 percent) would like to see "a central government for all Europeans," and a slight plurality (49 percent) supports an elected European head of state, a significant number oppose these two propositions (46 percent and 42 percent, respectively).[20] The outcome of the December 2000 EU Summit in Nice—where member states were only willing to make the bare minimum of progress toward streamlining the European Commission,

Figure 5-1.   *French Public Opinion on Support for and Benefit from EU Membership*[a]

a. Support for membership, 1981–2000

Percent

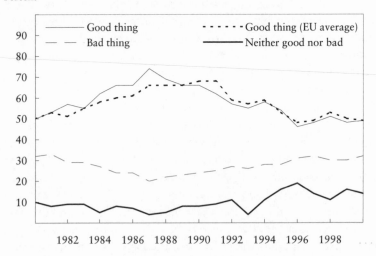

b. Benefit from membership, 1983–2000

Percent

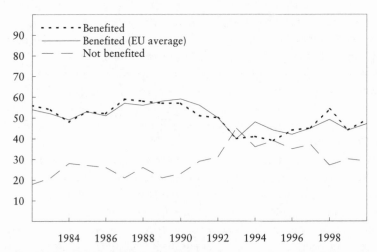

Source: European Union Directorate General for Education and Culture, "Standard Eurobarometer," 53 (Brussels, October 2000), figures 2-3 and 2-4, p. 16.

a. Percentage who answered "don't know" is not shown.

advancing qualified majority voting, and linking voting power to population size—was arguably an indication that there are limits to the degree of federalism EU leaders are prepared to accept.[21] What French leaders are prepared to accept, however—indeed what they are deeply committed to—is a union that uses its already considerable powers to forge a common European approach to globalization and its collective leverage to persuade the rest of the world to accept that approach. For most of the French, there really is no other choice.

Trade Policy

Another key tool that the French—and other Europeans—seek to use to manage the effects of globalization is trade policy. Trade is no longer a national responsibility for European countries but an EU responsibility, on which all member states have agreed to speak with a single voice.[22] The French, however, have always played an influential role in the formulation of common EU trade positions, and they continue to see this as one of their most important contributions to *mondialisation maîtrisée*. France, in fact, was a key force in the collective decision to transform the looser General Agreement on Tariffs and Trade (GATT), which had existed since 1947, into a World Trade Organization (WTO) with more binding rules and mechanisms to resolve disputes in January 1995.

Indeed, trade negotiations now go well beyond the discussion of tariff and nontariff barriers to the free circulation of goods and services; they also include issues such as workers' rights, the environment, health, food safety, and many other "new" areas that directly touch citizens' interests. Thus as part of its agenda of managing globalization, the EU has since the late 1990s been strongly advocating a new round of multilateral trade negotiations with a broad agenda, including rule making for investment, competition, trade and environment, social norms, and public procurement.[23] The Millennium Round, which was supposed to have been launched in Seattle in December 1999 (but stalled because leaders could not agree), was a European initiative. Its failure, however, has not stopped the European Union from continuing to advocate a new round in which rules will be developed for these new areas of commercial interaction. The EU hopes to persuade developing countries to support such rules, which they opposed in Seattle, by offering them other types of concessions, such as the free access agreement that the EU announced for trade with the poorest countries in February 2001.[24] These concessions—increased financial aid and better commercial access for poorer countries—are themselves part of the EU's overall plan to minimize the negative effects of globalization.

During its EU presidency, France made clear its belief that trade policy must be used to curb globalization's more harmful effects. Its program for the presidency stated: "Globalization, although the engine of progress, involves obvious dangers, in that it tends to homogenize and standardize cultures, damage the environment and impair food safety, and bring about inequalities between developed and developing countries. The new round of multilateral negotiations should take on board these concerns, which were voiced in a very direct manner in Seattle."[25] The French EU trade commissioner, Pascal Lamy, is a strong believer in the benefits of free trade, but like the French government he believes that states have a key role to play in curbing some of the effects of the market. "Through globalization," Lamy argues, "market capitalism confirms its three fundamental, and indivisible, characteristics: its efficiency, its instability, and its inegalitarian nature. We need its efficiency; we can prevent its instability; we must correct its inequitable character." France and the EU have made a number of concrete proposals for developing harnesses for globalization in order, in Lamy's words, to "share more equitably [its] costs and benefits."[26]

First, the EU continues to insist that core labor standards should be included in any international trade agreement. Neoliberal proponents of globalization and free trade, of course, argue that such standards interfere with the proper functioning of the principle of comparative advantage and that if carried too far they will negate the very benefits that free trade is supposed to bring. France, however, with widespread support in the EU, sees a minimum of rules on health, safety, and working conditions as prerequisites for further trade liberalization, and a sine qua non for mustering political support for such agreements. For France, such social and labor norms should include, for example, a ban on multinational companies using child labor and forced labor. "*Maîtriser la mondialisation*" was in fact the theme of the June 2000 ministerial meeting of the Organization for Economic Cooperation and Development (OECD), which discussed ways to introduce guidelines for good corporate behavior for multinationals. The OECD member countries, as well as Argentina, Brazil, Chile, and Slovakia, agreed to the "OECD Guiding Principles on Multinational Companies," though they could not agree on sanctions to ensure the effective application of these measures.[27] The EU plans to raise this issue again in the next round of multilateral trade talks under the WTO.

Second, the EU is insisting, with strong French encouragement, on the creation of worldwide rules for competition policy. Their reasoning is that very large, if not monopolistic, companies (such as the imaginary "World Company" that the French satirical television show *Les Guignols* uses to gibe the United States) need to be kept in check by stringent regulations on competition lest they become excessively dominant in their markets. Whereas the United States favors national rules—arguing that examples like the government's suit against Microsoft show that the United States is willing to promote fair competition vigorously—the EU prefers a multi-lateral approach, preferably under the WTO.[28]

Third, the EU plans to use the instruments already existing under WTO rules to control what is currently perceived as U.S. trade unilateralism— and has undoubtedly fueled the antiglobalization movement in France. Even as the WTO remains a target of antiglobalization protesters, who see it as fostering the open trade that they oppose, French and European leaders see it as one of the main tools with which they can curb the down-sides of globalization. Notwithstanding the WTO rulings against Europe on bananas and beef, the EU remains a leading user of the WTO dispute settlement procedures to enforce multilateral trade obligations. Indeed, several recent rulings against the United States, such as that calling for amendment of the foreign sales corporation scheme (the U.S. tax subsidy described above), have reinforced the Europeans' belief in the utility of multilateral trade regulations for making globalization operate more fairly.[29]

Fourth, the French are determined to put in place more stringent inter-national rules to ensure the safety of food that crosses borders. Whereas the United States has been reluctant to accept constraints on the freedom to export food—which Americans see as protectionism under the guise of precaution—the French and Europeans insist on a government's (in this case the EU's) sovereign right to do what it must to protect the health of its citizens. Pascal Lamy has been quite candid about the transatlantic difference: "On everything having to do with new materials like hormones, GMOs, etc., it is obvious that we do not at present have the same philoso-phy: in the United States these innovations are an opportunity, whereas in Europe we see them as more of a risk."[30] This perception of risk only increased over the course of 2001, with the continuation of the mad cow disease crisis; the appearance of genetically modified grains in batches of imported foods and fields from which it was supposed to have been banned; and finally, the development of foot and mouth disease, which effectively required quarantining the United Kingdom. As a result, the French are determined to maintain—and, if they can, to establish in international trade agreements—the notion of a "precautionary principle," which would give governments the right to block food imports whenever they felt that the health and safety of their citizens was at risk. France and the other Europeans won an important victory with the 2000 Montreal Biosafety Protocol, when the United States for the first time accepted the precautionary principle and the idea that all genetically modified foods should be labeled, but the transatlantic gap on such issues is still considerable.[31]

Finally, as has been seen, France is determined to cordon off cultural policy from the logic of free trade—the so-called cultural exception. Thanks to persistent French efforts during the 2000 Inter-Governmental Conference (IGC), culminating at Nice, the principle of the cultural exception is now enshrined in EU law. Despite strong pressure—including from Lamy and the rest of the European Commission—to extend qualified majority voting to trade in services and intellectual property issues (thereby eliminating the national veto), French leaders were adamant that it should not apply to trade in cultural goods. Doing so could mean an end to the quotas and subsidies that the French use to support their audiovisual and other cultural industries—a tacit admission that they are isolated on this point. The negotiations ended in a compromise that effectively extended qualified majority voting to most trade in services, but preserved the unanimity requirement for decisions regarding trade in cultural and audiovisual services—the cultural exception.[32] Notwithstanding its clear desire to persuade other countries to drop the veto right over areas of importance to them (the United Kingdom on tax harmonization and Germany on air transport, for example), France thus made it clear that it was willing to pay a high price to preserve its own ability to manage globalization in the cultural domain.

International Financial Regulation

One of the biggest concerns of the French about the implications of unregulated globalization is financial stability. This has in fact been one of the main issues in the debates about Europeanization for the past several decades, and particularly since the 1970s, as the development of new technology for transferring funds combined with the lifting of capital controls within the EU led to increased turbulence in financial markets. This turbu-

lence peaked in the early 1990s as unrestrained intra-EU capital movements in the wake of German unification forced several EU member states
to widen the fluctuation bands of the exchange rate mechanism (ERM) of
the European Monetary System (EMS), and others to abandon it all together. The EU's response to this ongoing challenge was the creation of
the euro, which, as already discussed, has provided the European economies with a significant degree of protection against the uncertainties of
international capital transfers.

In a world in which $1.5 trillion now exchanges hands every day, how-
ever, and when billions of dollars can be transferred around the world at
the touch of a button, France sees the need for greater global regulation to
prevent the sort of currency crises that struck Europe from occurring on a
global scale. These concerns were greatly increased, first, by the Mexican
peso crisis in 1995, when an overvalued currency and growing thirst for
imports led to a current account deficit, and eventually to the floating and
sharp depreciation of the currency. This was followed by the Asian financial crisis of 1997–98, which began in Thailand. As in Mexico, the combination of a fixed currency, rising imports, and a growing current account
deficit eventually forced the floating and devaluation of the Thai baht,
leading quickly to currency crises in other regional economies, such as
South Korea, Indonesia, and Malaysia, and to a lesser extent Hong Kong,
Taiwan, the Philippines, and Singapore. With investors now able to pull
their money out of a country as quickly as they had placed it there, the
crisis spread to other emerging economies in 1998 and took a particular
toll on Russia, where instability evokes in Europeans concern not just
about economics, but also immigration, energy security, and military security. The conclusion of many French people was that of economist and
Jospin adviser Jean-Paul Fitoussi: "A way must be found to bring the Fran-
kenstein of deregulated global markets under control."[33]

To do that, in September 1998, the French government developed a
far-reaching set of proposals for how to better govern the international
financial system. The result of close cooperation among the presidency,
the prime minister's office, and the Treasury (reflecting the French political consensus on this type of reform), the "Twelve Proposals for a European Initiative" became a key component of the French attempt to provide
rules for globalization.[34] It was also significant that France made these
proposals first to the European Union, seeking to take advantage of the
EU's weight in the world economy as well as of Europeans' sympathy for
measures to regulate globalization in the ways described above.

The French proposals were of two distinct sorts, the first of which was a series of ways in which Europe, acting on its own, could better contribute to global financial stability. These included closer coordination of economic policies within Europe (in particular, among the then eleven members of the Eurogroup); close transatlantic economic coordination; a European approach to persuade the United States to support ratification of an increase in the IMF capital base, as well as Europe's own willingness to provide exceptional financial resources so as to maintain the IMF's ability to act; extension of the area of monetary stability under the euro by persuading other EU countries to join the new ERM, and candidate countries to use the euro as a benchmark currency; and finally, encouragement of financial reforms in Russia, via the IMF and direct European assistance (including the Technical Assistance to the Commonwealth of Independent States [TACIS] program). Thus could the EU make a particular contribution to taming global financial markets.

The French initiative also included a set of proposals that would require broader international agreement, but for which France and Europe would fight. The most important of these was to institute "genuine political governance of the IMF," by which the French meant transforming the IMF's Interim Committee into a council—an authentic decisionmaking body that would meet on a more regular basis.[35] Dominique Strauss-Kahn, the French finance minister at the time, explained that "we need to have people with political responsibility more involved in the decisionmaking process. We need to have . . . a political body able to make decisions and to involve the ministers and the governments of the different countries much more closely in the decisions that are made."[36] The council would be responsible for promoting greater dialogue among developed and developing countries, and would work more closely with ministers and governments with political responsibility. Thus could it make real strategic choices and, with input from the World Bank, debate the social consequences of its adjustment programs.

Other elements of the French plan included greater disclosure and prudential supervision; more overseas development aid; cooperative responses to crises between the private sector and the IMF; a greater role for Europe under the euro; a more progressive and orderly approach to financial openness in developing countries, including a "financial safeguard clause" similar to Article 73 of the Maastricht Treaty. That article permits a six-month limit on capital flows during exceptional circumstances when there is a risk of capital movements causing serious harm.[37]

While the French proposals have found significant support in Europe, most of those requiring international consensus have not been agreed. As the international debate on how to take advantage of globalizing capital markets without increasing the potential for destabilizing crises—driven in part by the French proposals—proceeds, France will no doubt be among the leaders of those pushing for greater international regulation and control.

Managing Globalization through Foreign Policy

This book has concentrated primarily on the effects of globalization on France's economy, society, culture, and politics, but globalization also has an important geopolitical component, the implications of which the French are also seeking to manage. One implication is that as the world "shrinks"—because of falling transportation and communications costs, the spread of technology, the proliferation of ballistic missiles and weapons of mass destruction, and the growing ability of certain countries (primarily the United States) to project military power around the world—the scope for new types of international friction grows, creating the need to develop new tools for avoiding or limiting that friction. Although many countries, including France, have had international interests and responsibilities for centuries, the degree of their international interests and involvement—and the speed with which crises in one region can affect the interests of others—is greater now than ever before. Computer viruses; terrorism; threats to energy sources; refugee flows; communicable diseases like AIDS, tuberculosis, or mad cow disease; the collapse of export markets; currency crises; and the threat of ballistic missiles topped with weapons of mass destruction are just some of the security risks whose effects can be magnified by this aspect of globalization.

Even more salient to France is the tendency of globalization to strengthen the one power that benefits most from it: the United States. As Foreign Minister Hubert Védrine has argued, Americans derive particular benefits from globalization "because of their economic size; because globalization takes place in their language; because it is organized along neo-liberal economic principles; because they impose their legal, accounting and technical practices; and because they're advocates of individualism."[38] Védrine rightly believes that the power of the United States—already a "hyperpower"—is enhanced by globalization because it is able to take advantage of technology, it can adapt its economy flexibly, its language is becoming increasingly universal, and it can project its already dominant culture. France, which has never been willing to passively accept American leadership, now more than ever seeks to promote a multipolar world, in part to ensure that globalization and Americanization do not become one and the same.

The promotion of a multipolar world has been a key goal of French foreign policy since World War II, and especially after the end of the cold war and 1990–91 Gulf War left only a single superpower standing. As the globalization debate began to reach its peak in the late 1990s, French calls for multipolarity became even more insistent. At the November 1999 celebration of the twentieth anniversary of the French Institute of International Relations, for example, both Jacques Chirac and Hubert Védrine emphasized the need for alternatives to a world dominated by the United States alone. Chirac spoke of a U.S. Congress that "too often gave in to the temptations of unilateralism and isolationism," and Védrine insisted that France could not accept "a politically unipolar world, a culturally uniform world, or a world dominated by the lone superpower. This is why we are fighting for a world that is multipolar, diversified, and multilateral."[39]

One of the main ways in which France seeks to both limit American hegemony and reduce the security risks of globalization is by developing "rules" for the international system. Védrine justifies this, in part, as the defense of the weak against the strong: "The French government calls for more rules to frame globalization so that it doesn't only come down to a resuscitation of 'might makes right.'"[40] It was with reference not only to trade and finance but also to geopolitics that Jospin argued at a meeting of the United Nations (UN) General Assembly in September 1999 that "the more the world globalizes, the more it needs rules."[41] By *rules*, France means binding international agreements, focused first and foremost on the United Nations charter and its Security Council (UNSC) resolutions. Thus, whereas the United States seeks to preserve NATO's right to intervene militarily, even without UN Security Council resolutions (as in Kosovo, for example), France insists that a UN mandate is necessary to provide legality and legitimacy to such operations (although it was prepared to make Kosovo an exception to the general rule). This was a major area of contention between France and the United States during the negotiation of NATO's new Strategic Concept in 1999; a compromise was eventually reached by including language that referred to the NATO allies' "commitment to the UN Charter" and the "primacy of the United Nations Security Council," but omitting explicit reference to the need for a UN mandate.[42]

Policy toward Iraq is another important area where France has appealed to UNSC resolutions and international law as constraints on American freedom of action. Whereas the United States has on occasion made clear that it would not lift sanctions on Iraq so long as Saddam Hussein remains in power, France has insisted that the letter of UNSC resolution 687 must be adhered to—meaning that sanctions would have to be lifted if that resolution's conditions (primarily, the elimination of Iraq's long-range ballistic missiles and weapons of mass destruction) were met.[43] Likewise, when American and British jets bombed Iraqi radar stations near Baghdad in February 2001 to enforce their self-declared "no-fly zones," Védrine criticized their actions for having "no basis in international law."[44]

France's emphasis of the need for international rules to govern globalization reflects a recognition of its limited power relative to the United States, whose hyperpower status makes it far less averse to a world in which "might makes right." This dynamic—France's greater support for rules, international law, and multilateralism—goes well beyond the United Nations framework. French support for the International Criminal Court set up in 2000 (belatedly signed and still not ratified by the United States), the Kyoto treaty on climate change (rejected in March 2001 by President George W. Bush), the international land mines protocol (not signed by the United States), arms control agreements like the 1972 Anti-Ballistic Missile Treaty (called into question by the U.S. ballistic missile defense program) and the 1999 Comprehensive Nuclear Test Ban Treaty (not ratified by the United States and opposed by Bush), and France's strong reactions against the secondary sanctions provisions of the Libertad Act and Iran-Libya Sanctions Act (evidencing U.S. attempts to impose its laws on others) are all further examples of France's strong desire to govern geopolitical globalization, and constrain American unilateralism, with binding rules.

As a final rampart against the potential security risks of globalization dominated by the United States, the French, as noted above, seek to develop the European Union as a political—as opposed to merely a commercial—power. Chirac explains the pursuit of EU integration as states coming together "in response to globalization . . . to preserve, on a regional scale, control over their own fate."[45] Indeed, 56 percent of the French public sees Europe as useful for enhancing "French influence in the world," compared with just 13 percent who think the opposite.[46] Promotion of a Europe with political and security responsibilities is an old theme for France;

it was part of the Fourth Republic's logic in launching the European Community, and it was certainly a goal of de Gaulle in the 1960s (albeit in both cases the assumption was that this strategic Europe would be led by France). Today, it takes the form of the European Union's Common Foreign and Security Policy (CFSP), launched at Maastricht in 1991 and advanced in Amsterdam in 1997 with the appointment of Javier Solana as high representative for the Common Foreign and Security Policy, a position France strongly supported as a way of giving more visibility to CFSP. Furthermore, at the Franco-British summit in Saint Malo in December 1998, the British (to the delight of the French) accepted the long-standing French goal of giving the European Union the capacity for the autonomous use of military force.[47] This objective was codified at the Cologne, Helsinki, Feira, and Nice European Councils from June 1999 through December 2000, with agreement on a European Security and Defense Policy (ESDP), the establishment of EU security policymaking institutions, and the creation of the military "headline goal"—the capacity to assemble 60,000 EU troops within two months and deploy them for at least a year. With these tools at its disposal, Europe might be on its way to becoming the sort of political and diplomatic power the French have for so long sought to build.[48]

The promotion of a multipolar world, strong backing for international laws and agreements, and the vigorous promotion of a political Europe with tools for military power are examples of the *volontariste* state at work in the foreign policy domain. Just as trade and social policy and European integration are designed to shield France from globalization's social and economic effects, the promotion of multilateralism and the ESDP are designed to cushion the geopolitical and strategic effects of a globalized world dominated by a single superpower.

Responding to Globalization the French Way

It is easy to caricature the French response to globalization as the resistance of an old-fashioned, somewhat backward country struggling to adapt to the modern world. What with José Bové, *Le Monde Diplomatique,* the rhetoric of many French politicians, and the array of interventionist measures that fall under the heading of *"mondialisation maîtrisée,"* France sometimes gives the impression that it wishes globalization would just go away. From an American point of view, in particular, many of France's policies—the interventionist and economically costly thirty-five-hour work week, tariffs and quotas on "cultural goods," proposals to constrain the development of global trade and investment, and opposition to U.S. global leadership, to name just a few—represent a "typically French" attempt to interfere with the natural development of global progress, presumably toward a world based on "American" principles of individualism, economic liberalism, and Washington's diplomatic leadership. This view is not entirely wrong. As this book has demonstrated, globalization is a direct challenge to many aspects of French political, cultural, and economic tradition, and adapting to it requires the kinds of profound social changes that are never easy to accept.

A closer look at the French response to globalization, however, reveals a much more nuanced picture. Perhaps most important, France's adaptation to globalization—particularly but not exclusively in the economic domain—goes much deeper than most observers recognize, and even than most French politicians are prepared to admit to a still nervous public. As seen in chapter 2, the French economy is now one of the most globally integrated in the world, *dirigisme* is becoming a thing of the past, French companies and business leaders are accommodating to the practices of the "new economy," and the economy has been thriving as a result. Other changes, such as the rise of nongovernmental organizations, politically active business leaders, more aggressive investigative journalists, magistrates who are not afraid of the state and political class, and new social norms (for example, affirmative action and homosexual partnerships), have also been promoted by influences coming from abroad and are having a real impact on French society. The French may not be willing to embrace all the implications of globalization, but they have been affected by many of them.

While France still has a long way to go in making the changes necessary to deal with globalization, Americans should also remember that the United States did not immediately embrace globalization when it started to develop in the 1980s. The U.S. ambassador to France from 1997 to 2000, former investment banker Felix Rohatyn, has made this point eloquently:

> While we watch countries like France struggle to adjust their culture and their politics to both the pressures and benefits of globalization, we have a tendency to forget our own reactions to globalization just ten years ago. In the 1980s, it looked like Japan and Germany were going to take over the world; fierce international competition was forcing management changes and large restructurings at our most

important companies. Anti-takeover statutes were rushed through our legislatures in state after state to protect American companies from hostile takeovers, both foreign and domestic. But we stayed the course, modernized our economy, and created the conditions for unparalleled growth.[49]

If the French economy continues to adapt at anything like its pace for the past fifteen years, the differences between the once-unique "French model" and the economic practices of other Europeans, and even the United States, will continue to shrink.

It remains to be seen whether it will continue to adapt, and whether French leaders will manage to strike the right balance between "mastering" globalization and taking advantage of it. So far they have largely succeeded, but as long as the French people remain skeptical about globalization and French leaders are unwilling to admit the limits of their ability to control it, the possibility of a reversal cannot be excluded. Indeed, such skepticism intensified in France in the late 1990s—a period of extraordinary prosperity, job creation, and economic growth. Should that favorable economic climate change for the worse, especially in the context of the upcoming presidential and parliamentary elections, with nonmainstream parties on both sides attacking economic liberalism, French politicians might feel obliged to accommodate antiglobalization sentiments even more than at present. This would not only have negative consequences for French economic prospects and political stability, but, given that globalization is so frequently equated with Americanization, it would no doubt spill over in a negative way to transatlantic relations. Hence the importance for French political and intellectual leaders today not only to stress that globalization must be tamed, but equally, to acknowledge the benefits that it can bring.

As outsiders assess France's particular approach to globalization, and even as they watch the French struggle with it, they should keep an open mind about aspects of the French approach that might be worthy of consideration. The simple notion that "more globalization is better," as if there were some natural, linear developmental trajectory with the United States as the ultimate example of successful adaptation should not be accepted uncritically. That France embraces some elements of globalization while rejecting or seeking to modify others is not necessarily evidence of schizophrenia or hypocrisy, but perhaps just a sign of the only way France can gradually domesticate—and persuade its public to accept—a phenomenon that challenges its political and economic traditions.

With the French Revolution, more than two hundred years ago, France set out to carry a "universal" message—the foundation of democracy and human rights—across Europe and then around the world. It may be too much to suggest that "managed globalization" will become the twenty-first century equivalent of the Declaration of the Rights of Man, but the French approach does present an alternative to the view that globalization signals the death of the nation state and that governments no longer have a crucial role to play in the lives of their citizens. As the world confronts a phenomenon that, as the French so often point out, combines enormous power to do good with the potential for creating great inequality and uncertainty, France's case for *mondialisation maîtrisée* should be welcomed rather than condemned.

Notes

Chapter 1

1. See, for example, Suzanne Daley, "French Turn Vandal into Hero against U.S.," *New York Times*, July 1, 2000, p. A1; Eric Aeschimann, "Il était une foi nommée Bové," *Libération*, June 30, 2000; Robert Belleret, "José Bové ou le goût du contre-pouvoir," *Le Monde*, January 1, 2000; and William Abitbol and Paul-Marie Couteaux, "Souverainisme, j'écris ton nom," *Le Monde*, September 30, 1999.

2. See the results of the July 2001 Sofres poll published as "Une menace ou une chance?" *Le Monde*, July 19, 2001, p. 3; BVA, "L'impact de la mondialisation," September 1999 (www.bva.fr/archives/mondialisation9940.html [June 2001]); Canal Ispos, "Mondialisation: les Français ont le trac," September 18–19, 1998 (www.canalipsos.com/cap/sondage/result2.cfm?choix=98207 [June 2001]); and Eric Dupin, "Les limites du libéralisme français," Canal Ipsos (www.canalipsos.com/articles_fr/9908/nllefrance.htm [June 2001]).

3. In the question about sympathy and support, 37 percent were indifferent and 14 percent did not respond. The survey was a telephone poll of 1,000 French people aged eighteen and over. See "L'attitude des Français à l'égard de José Bové

et ses prises de position," June 28–29 2000, CSA, June 30, 2000 (www.csa-tmo.fr/fra/dataset/data2k/opi20000629a.htm [June 2001]).

4. The expression *la malbouffe* seems to have first been used in 1981 in a book by Stella and Joël de Rosnay, but it was Bové who popularized the term. See Stella de Rosnay and Joël de Rosnay, *La Malbouffe* (Paris: Seuil, Points-Actuels, 1981); and José Bové and François Dufour, *Le Monde n'est pas une marchandise: des paysans contre la malbouffe* (Paris: Editions La Découverte, 2000), esp. pp. 77–78.

5. See Viviane Forrester, *L'Horreur économique* (Paris: Fayard, 1996); Viviane Forrester, *Une Etrange Dictature* (Paris: Fayard, 1999); Bové and Dufour, *Le Monde n'est pas une marchandise*. Among many other examples—some of which attack capitalism, if not globalization per se—one might include Emmanuel Todd, *L'Illusion économique* (Paris: Gallimard, 1998); Philippe Labarde and Bernard Maris, *Ah Dieu! Que la guerre économique est jolie!* (Paris: Albin Michel, 1998); Noel Mamère and Olivier Warin, "Non merci, Oncle Sam!" (Paris: Ramsay, 1999); Pierre Bourdieu, *Contre-feux* (Paris: Liber/Raisons d'agir, 1998); and Pierre Bourdieu, *Les Structures sociales de l'économie* (Paris: Le Seuil, 2000).

6. These three programs appeared in a single week, on different stations, in March 2000.

7. See Babette Stern, "Diplomatie Compassionnelle," *Le Monde*, May 16, 2001.

8. Authors' calculations based on a search of the Foreign Broadcast Information Service (FBIS) database.

9. To cite only a few of the more recent: Bernard Cassen, "Non, la mondialisation n'est pas 'heureuse'," *Le Monde*, August 24, 2001, pp. 1, 11; Alain Minc, "Mondialisation heureuse: je persiste et signe," *Le Monde*, August 17, 2001, pp. 1, 10; Jacques Chirac, "Humaniser la mondialisation," *Le Figaro*, July 19, 2001, pp. 1, 10; Edouard Balladur, "Pour une mondialisation organisée," *Le Monde*, April 13, 2001; Lionel Jospin, "Maîtriser la mondialisation," *Les Echos*, April 10, 2001; Jean-Marie Messier, "Vivre la diversité culturelle," *Le Monde*, April 10, 2001; Jean-Claude Gayssot, "Du bon usage de la mondialisation," *Libération*, May 14, 2001; Pascal Lamy, "Une mondialisation solidaire," *Libération*, May 16, 2001; and André Fourçans, "Peut-on réguler la mondialisation?" *Le Figaro*, May 17, 2001.

10. See "M. Jospin dénonce une 'mondialisation débridée,'" *Le Monde*, January 3, 2000; and "Le Discours de Lionel Jospin à Rio," *Le Monde*, April 18, 2001.

11. See John Tagliabue, "Resisting the Ugly Americans: Contempt in France for U.S. Funds and Investors," *New York Times*, January 9, 2000, sec. 3, p. 1.

12. See, for example, Jacques Chirac's speech to the Institut Français des Relations Internationales (IFRI) on November 4, 1999, published as "La France dans un monde multipolaire," *Politique Etrangère* (Winter 1999–2000), pp. 803–12.

13. See Hubert Védrine's speech to IFRI on November 4, 1999, published as "Le Monde au Tournant du Siècle," *Politique Etrangère* (Winter 1999–2000), p. 819.

14. See, for example, Sophie Meunier, "The French Exception," *Foreign Affairs* (July–August 2000), pp. 104–16; and Pierre Rosanvallon, "France: The New Anti-Capitalism," *Correspondence: An International Review of Culture and Society*, vol. 7 (Winter 2000–01), pp. 34–35.

15. See Erik Izraelewicz, *Le Capitalism zinzin* (Paris: Grasset, 1999), p. 13; and Adrien de Tricornot, "Qui sont les propriétaires des entreprises européennes?" *Le Monde*, June 15, 2001.

16. See *World Development Indicators*, CD-ROM (Washington: World Bank, 2000).

17. See the discussion in chapter 2 below, as well as Sylvie Hattemer-Lefèvre, "Ces Entreprises qui se moquent de la France," *Le Nouvel Economiste*, May 31, 2000; and Philip H. Gordon, "The Tale of José Bové and Vivendi," SpeakOut.com, July 10, 2000.

18. Growth was 3.3 percent in 1998 and 3.2 percent in both 1999 and 2000. See Lamia Oualalou, "La France reste la locomotive de l'Europe," *Le Figaro: Economie I*, February 24, 2001.

19. *Le Monde: Bilan du Monde, Edition 2001* (Paris: Le Monde, 2001), pp. 140–41.

20. France's main stock market index, the CAC 40, declined by less than 1/2 percent in 2000, compared with drops of 5 percent in the U.S. Dow Jones industrial average, 10 percent in Britain's FTSE 100, and 27 percent in Japan's Nikkei 225. See Gary Silverman and Alex Skorecki, "FTSE Fall Sharpest in Decade: Backlash over TMT Stocks and Slowing American Economy Blamed," *Financial Times*, December 30, 2000, p. 1.

21. See Isabelle Mandraud, "La baisse du chômage se poursuit au ralenti," *Le Monde*, April 28, 2001; *Le Monde: Bilan du Monde*, p. 137; and "French Job Growth Is Most in 3 Decades," *International Herald-Tribune*, March 11–12, 2000.

22. See "Portrait d'une France en pleine croissance," *Le Monde*, January 9, 2001; also, the highly favorable portrait of the French economy by the Organization for Economic Cooperation and Development, *OECD Economic Surveys: France* (Paris, July 2000).

23. See, for example, Kenneth N. Waltz, "Globalization and American Power," *National Interest*, vol. 59 (Spring 2000), pp. 46–56; Michael D. Bordo, Barry Eichengreen, and Douglas A. Irwin, "Is Globalization Today Really Different from Globalization a Hundred Years Ago?" in Susan M. Collins and Robert Z. Lawrence, eds., *Brookings Trade Forum 1999* (Brookings, 1999), pp. 1–72; and Ellen L. Frost, "Globalization and National Security: A Strategic Agenda," in Richard L. Kugler and Ellen L. Frost, eds., *The Global Century: Globalization and National Security* (Washington: National Defense University Press, 2001), pp. 35–74.

24. See Thomas L. Friedman, *The Lexus and the Olive Tree: Understanding Globalization* (Farrar, Straus and Giroux, 1999), pp. xiii–xvi. For other good comparisons between the two eras, see Dani Rodrik, "Has Globalization Gone too Far?" *California Management Review*, vol. 39 (Spring 1997), pp. 34–36; Jeffrey Frankel, "Globalization of the Economy," in Joseph S. Nye Jr. and John D. Donahue, eds., *Governance in a Globalizing World* (Brookings, 2000), pp. 45–50; John Micklethwait and Adrian Wooldridge, *A Future Perfect: The Challenge and Hidden Promise of Globalization* (Crown, 2000), pp. 3–25; and Bordo, Eichengreen, and Irwin, "Is Globalization Today Really Different from Globalization a Hundred Years Ago?"

25. See United Nations, *World Investment Report 2000* (New York and Geneva, 2000), pp. xv–xviii; World Trade Organization, *International Trade Statistics*

2000 (Geneva, 2000), app. tabs. A3–A6, p. 164–77; and the statistics provided in A. T. Kearney, "Measuring Globalization," *Foreign Policy* (January–February 2001), pp. 56–65. Other useful indicators of the recent growth and current extent of globalization can be found in Micklethwait and Wooldrige, *A Future Perfect*, p. xxi.

26. See, for example, the discussion in Frankel, "Globalization of the Economy," pp. 45–46.

27. See Robert O. Keohane and Joseph S. Nye Jr., "Introduction," in Nye and Donahue, *Governance in a Globalizing World*, p. 2.

28. Ibid., p. 6.

29. See the OECD figures in Documentation française, *Rapport Annuel* (Paris, March 1998–99). According to the Institut National de la Statistique et des Etudes Economiques (INSEE), the French state at all levels, including the education and health care systems, the military, and state-run services such as the postal service and parts of France Télécom, employed 5.4 million people as of 1998. This was some 20 percent of the "active population" (including the unemployed) and 22.5 percent of those actually in work. See INSEE, *Tableaux de l'Economie Française* (Paris, 2000), p. 82.

30. See Jean-Jacques Servan-Schreiber, *Le Défi américain* (Paris: Editions Denoel, 1967), published in English as *The American Challenge* (New York: Atheneum, 1968 [translated by Ronald Steel]).

31. See, for example, Serge Berstein and Odile Rudelle, *Le Modèle républicain* (Paris: Presses Universitaires de France, 1992); and Régis Debray's essay "République ou Démocratie" in his book *Contretemps: Eloge des idéaux perdus* (Paris: Gallimard, 1992), pp. 15–54. Also, see the concise discussion in Stanley Hoffmann's preface to Charles Cogan, *Oldest Allies, Guarded Friends: The United States and France since 1940* (Westport, Conn.: Praeger, 1994), pp. vii–ix, and Cogan's own discussion on pp. 8–15.

32. For a recent discussion, see Philip H. Gordon, "The French Position," *National Interest* (Fall 2000), pp. 57–65.

33. See Department of State, Office of Research, "West Europeans Tend to View Globalization Positively," European Opinion Alert, November 20, 2000.

34. See Dominique Moïsi, "The Trouble with France," *Foreign Affairs*, vol. 77 (May–June 1998), p. 97.

35. See Hubert Védrine, with Dominique Moïsi, *France in an Age of Globalization* (Brookings, 2001), pp. 17–18. This is an updated and expanded English-language version of Védrine's *Les Cartes de la France à l'heure de la mondialisation* (Paris: Fayard, 2000).

Chapter 2

1. Cited in "M. Jospin dénonce une 'mondialisation débridée'," *Le Monde*, January 4, 2000; and Martin Walker, "Jospin's Tightrope," Intellectual Capital.com, October 14, 1999.

2. See, for example, Dominique Moïsi, "The Trouble with France," *Foreign Affairs*, vol. 77 (May–June 1998); and David R. Cameron, "National Interest, the

Dilemmas of European Integration, and Malaise," in John T. S. Keeler and Martin A. Schain, eds., *Chirac's Challenge: Liberalization, Europeanization and Malaise in France* (St. Martin's Press, 1996), pp. 325–81.

3. See "Portrait d'une France en pleine croissance," *Le Monde,* January 9, 2001; Lamia Oualalou, "Les ménages français plus optimistes que jamais," *Le Figaro,* July 6, 2000; Patrick Jarreau, "Sortie de crise," *Le Monde,* August 4, 2000; and Jean-Michel Bezat and Pascale Robert-Diard, "Enquête sur une France optimiste," *Le Monde,* July 31, 2000.

4. This notion has been evoked in Tony Barber, "Changing Places," *Financial Times,* February 23, 2000; Lamia Oualalou, "La France reste la locomotive de l'Europe," *Le Figaro,* February 24, 2001, Section Economie, p. 1; and Marie-France Calle, "L'Allemagne reléguée au second rang," *Le Figaro,* February 24–25, 2001, Section Economie, p. 1.

5. See Peter Hall, *Governing the Economy: The Politics of State Intervention in Britain and France* (Oxford University Press, 1986), p. 141; Vivien A. Schmidt, *From State to Market? The Transformation of French Business and Government* (Cambridge University Press, 1996); and Jonah Levy, *Tocqueville's Revenge: State, Society and Economy in Contemporary France* (Harvard University Press, 1999).

6. See Richard Kuisel, *Capitalism and the State in Modern France: Renovation and Economic Management* (Cambridge University Press, 1981); and Andrew Shonfield, *Modern Capitalism* (Oxford University Press, 1969).

7. See Hall, *Governing the Economy,* p. 141; Schmidt, *From State to Market?*; and Levy, *Tocqueville's Revenge.*

8. See Hall, *Governing the Economy,* p. 167.

9. These figures are from the Organization for Economic Cooperation and Development and the International Monetary Fund, cited in Jean-François Molinari, "Le poids des dépenses publiques ne cesse d'augmenter," *Le Figaro,* March 3, 2000.

10. See Le Monde, *Bilan Economique et Social 2000* (Paris, 2000), p. 142; Gaël Dupont and Vincent Touzé, "Réforme de la Fiscalité," in Observatoire Français des Conjonctures Economiques (OFCE), *L'économie française 2001* (Paris: La Découverte, 2001), p. 97; Bérengère Mathieu de Heaulme, "Les prélèvements obligatoires à 45.8%," *Le Figaro,* March 3, 2000; and Marie-Laetitia Bonavita, "Baisse de la pression fiscale: Jospin rate ses objectifs," *Le Figaro,* March 10–11, 2001.

11. See French Presidency of the European Union, "L'économie: la politique économique" (www.presidence-europe.fr/pfue/dossiers/00269-ct/fr/eco01.html [June 13, 2001]).

12. See René Rémond, *Les Droites en France* (Paris: Aubier Montaigne, 1982), pp. 290–312.

13. See Volkmar Lauber, *The Political Economy of France* (Praeger, 1983), p. 102.

14. The state also repurchased the remaining private shares in the state-controlled banks Crédit Lyonnais, Banque Nationale de Paris, and Société Générale and purchased a major stake in two defense firms, Dassault and Matra. See Hall, *Governing the Economy,* p. 202–06; Schmidt, *From State to Market?* pp. 114–

18; and Julius W. Friend, *The Long Presidency: France in the Mitterrand Years, 1981–1995* (Boulder, Colo.: Westview Press, 1998), pp. 28–30.

15. For details on Mitterrand's policies, see Hall, *Governing the Economy*, pp. 193–95.

16. See John Ardagh, *France in the New Century* (London: Viking, 1999), p. 77.

17. For trade as a share of the national economy, see Penn World Tables, version 5.6 (http://pwt.econ.upenn.edu [June 13, 2001). See also figure 2-3 below.

18. For a good account of this period, see Pierre Favier and Michel Martin-Roland, *La Décennie Mitterrand*, vol., 1, *Les ruptures (1981–1984)* (Paris: Seuil, 1990), pp. 401–93. For analysis, see Hall, *Governing the Economy*, pp. 192–226; and Patrick McCarthy, "France Faces Reality: *Rigueur* and the Germans," in David P. Calleo and Claudia Morgenstern, eds., *Recasting Europe's Economies: National Strategies in the 1980s* (Lanham, Md.: University Press of America, 1990), p. 67.

19. See Erik Izraelewicz, *Le Capitalisme zinzin* (Paris: Bernard Grasset, 1999), p. 120.

20. See "Un mouvement amplifié à partir de 1993," *Le Monde*, December 29, 2000; and "A Survey of France: The Grand Illusion," *Economist*, June 5, 1999, p. 6.

21. See Jérome Jaffré, "La gauche accepte le marché, la droite admet la différence," *Le Monde*, August 15, 1999.

22. See Virginie Malingre and Laurent Maudit, "Privatisation, la nouvelle controverse," *Le Monde*, December 29, 2000.

23. See the arguments of Robert Hue (Communist Party), Henri Emanuelli (Socialist Party), and Jean-Pierre Chevènement (Mouvement des Citoyens) in "Faut-il encore privatiser?" *Le Monde*, December 29, 2000.

24. Cited in Bérengère Mathieu de Heaulme, "Un ministre qui a cultivé les patrons," *Le Figaro*, March 29, 2000, Section Economie, p. 4.

25. See Izraelewicz, *Le Capitalisme zinzin*, p. 137.

26. See Philippe Manière, *Marx à la Corbeille: Quand les actionnaires font la Révolution* (Paris: Stock, 1999).

27. See Jean-Marie Messier, *J6M.com: Faut-il avoir peur de la nouvelle économie?* (Paris: Hachette, 2000), p. 28.

28. On France's financial reform of the 1980s, see Michael Loriaux, *France after Hegemony: International Change and Financial Reform* (Cornell University Press, 1991).

29. Izraelewicz, *Le Capitalisme zinzin*, p. 151. Also see "Coup de jeune pour l'actionnariat français," *Le Figaro*, July 5, 2000.

30. 20.5 percent of those over fifteen years old. The figures are taken from a study by the Banque de France and ParisBourse. See "Les Français retrouvent le chemin de la Bourse," *Le Monde*, July 6, 2000; and "Coup de Jeune pour l'actionnariat français."

31. See Adrien de Tricornot, "Qui sont les propriétaires des entreprises européennes?" *Le Monde*, June 15, 2001; and John Tagliabue, "Resisting Those Ugly Americans: Contempt in France for U.S. Funds and Investors," *New York*

Times, January 9, 2000, sec. 3, p. 1. Former U.S. ambassador to France Felix Rohatyn estimates that 30 to 40 percent of French securities are owned by "Anglo-American financial institutions," amounting to between $300 billion and $500 billion. See Felix G. Rohatyn, "The U.S., Europe and Globalization," remarks delivered at the Université d'Auvergne, Clermont-Ferrand, France (www.useu.be/issues/rohat0512/html).

32. See Izraelewicz, *Le Capitalism zinzin*, pp. 13, 195.

33. See Anne Swardson and David Dunn, "Europe's Entrepreneurial Allure Attracts American Investors," *Washington Post*, February 13, 2000, p. H5; and Cait Murphy, "The Next French Revolution," *Fortune*, June 12, 2000, p. 162.

34. One of the reasons for this is that France got a relatively early start in developing the use of stock options, under Finance Minister Edouard Balladur during France's "neoliberal" interlude of 1986–88. See Jean-Pierre Ponssard, "Stock Options and Performance-Based Pay in France," *U.S.-France Analysis* (Brookings Center on the United States and France, February 2001). Also see "Enquête sur les stock-options," *Le Monde*, March 5, 2001; Virginie Malingre, "La France en deuxième position mondiale pour les stock-options," *Le Monde*, September 14, 2000; Robert Graham, "The Soft-Option." *Financial Times*, April 28, 2000, p. 18; and Laurent Mauduit, "Stock-options: un succès fulgurant dans les plus grandes sociétés françaises," *Le Monde*, September 8, 1999.

35. See Virginie Malingre and Michel Noblecourt, "Les députés PS veulent taxer davantage les stock-options," *Le Monde*, October 14, 1999; and Jean-Michel Bezat and Virginie Malingre, "M. Strauss-Kahn se résigne à alourdir la fiscalité des stock-options," *Le Monde*, October 22, 1999.

36. Specifically, the minimum period for being able to exercise stock options is lowered from five to four years, but the existing tax rate of 40 percent will apply for capital gains of 1 million francs if the shares are held for six years, and at 50 percent if held only for five years. Gains below 1 million francs will be taxed at 26 percent. These new rates will apply to stock option gains made after 2004. See "French Parliament Clears Stock Option Tax," *Financial Times,* April 28, 2000; and Jean-Michel Bezat, "La nouvelle fiscalité des stock-options ne sera effective qu'en avril 2004," *Le Monde*, April 29, 2000.

37. See Philippe Manière, "Le Retour des patrons français," *Le Point*, June 23, 2000; and David Woodruff, "French Firms Embrace Capitalism despite Government Intervention," *Wall Street Journal*, November 24, 1999, p. A15.

38. See Sylvie Hattemer-Lefèvre, "Ces entreprises qui se moquent de la France," *Le Nouvel Economiste*, May 31, 2000, p. 52.

39. See Messier, *J6M.com*, p. 33; and Pascal Galinier, "Ces patrons qui menent l'offensive," *Le Monde*, January 1, 2000.

40. Thomson Financial Securities Data, cited in Murphy, "The Next French Revolution," p. 162.

41. The Alcatel-Lucent deal subsequently fell through, but the fact that it was attempted indicates French companies' interest in external expansion. See "French Investment Abroad: Behind the Bluster," *Economist,* May 26, 2001, pp. 58, 61; and Andrew Ross Sorkin, "Vivendi to Buy MP3.com to Expand on the Internet," *International Herald-Tribune*, May 22, 2001, p. 15.

42. See Ardagh, *France in the New Century*, pp. 83–84; and John Rossant, "France's Yank-Bashing Is Getting Sillier and Sillier," *Business Week*, March 13, 2000, p. 56.

43. See Clifford Krauss, "Selling to Argentina," *New York Times*, December 5, 1999, sec. 3, p. 7.

44. See Tom Buerkle, "A Big Leap for Banking in Europe," *International Herald-Tribune*, April 3, 2000, p. 1.

45. Jean-Luc Bardet, "L'intervention des pouvoirs publiques dans la bataille des banques," Agence France-Presse, August 20, 1999.

46. See Laure Belot and Pascal Galinier, "Le gouvernement invoque la libre concurrence pour s'opposer à la reprise d'Orangina par Coca-Cola," *Le Monde*, September 19, 1999.

47. See the interview with Thierry Desmarest, "France Is Changing Rapidly," *Business Week*, September 27, 1999, p. 33. Similarly, Messier points out that when he was negotiating possible mergers between Vivendi and U.K. and German companies, he "did not for a minute think of going to see a government minister or some high-level bureaucrat to keep him informed of the negotiations." See Messier, *J6M.com*, p. 40.

48. See Suzanne Berger, "Trade and Identity: The Coming Protectionism?" in Gregory Flynn, ed., *Remaking the Hexagon: The New France in the New Europe* (Boulder, Colo.: Westview Press, 1995), p. 196.

49. See Jean Arthuis, "Rapport d'information fait au nom de la commission des finances, du contrôle budgétaire et des comptes économiques de la Nation sur l'incidence économique et fiscale des délocalisations hors du territoire national des activités industrielles et de service," no. 337, Sénat, Seconde Session Ordinaire de 1992–93.

50. See Berger, "Trade and Identity," p. 197; and Elie Cohen, *La Tentation hexagonale: La Souveraineté à l'épreuve de la mondialisation* (Paris: Fayard, 1996), pp. 123–32.

51. For example, as Suzanne Berger has pointed out, although textiles and the garment industry were allegedly key culprits in the loss of French jobs, only 2.7 percent of overall French foreign investment was in these industries, and of that, only 4.1 percent went to non-OECD countries. It is hard to believe that 0.001 percent of French FDI is responsible for a significant loss of French jobs. See Berger, "Trade and Identity," p. 198; and Jean-Pierre Tuquoi, "Ne pas céder aux sirènes du protectionnisme," *Le Monde*, October 2, 1993, p. 27.

52. See "Edouard Balladur défend sa politique économique," *Le Monde*, June 20–21, 1993.

53. See *World Development Indicators 2000*, CD-ROM (Washington: World Bank, 2000).

54. See Patrick Messerlin, "France and Trade Policy: Is the French Exception *Passée?*" *International Affairs*, vol. 72 (April 1996), pp. 293–309.

55. For a good discussion, see David R. Cameron, "From Barre to Balladur," in Flynn, *Remaking the Hexagon*, pp. 117–37.

56. See Institut National de la Statistique et des Etudes Economiques (INSEE), *Tableaux de l'économie française 2000/2001* (Paris, 2000), p. 187.

57. Cited in Tony Barber, "Changing Places," *Financial Times,* February 23, 2000, p. 22.

58. See Tom Buerkle, "Schroeder Triggers Sinking of Euro to a Record Low," *International Herald-Tribune,* September 7, 2000, p. 1.

59. See Barber, "Changing Places."

60. See Marie-Laetitia Bonavita and Bérengère Mathieu de Heaulme, "Pression fiscale record," *Le Figaro,* March 3, 2000. The gap between state spending (around 54 percent) and the tax burden (46 percent) can be explained by the government deficit (nearly 3 percent of GDP) as well as the combination of income received by the state from sales of goods and services, interest from state-owned properties, and various other transfers, adding up to around 5 percent of GDP. We would like to thank economist Patrick Messerlin for clarification of this point.

61. See Organization for Cooperation and Development (OECD), *OECD Economic Surveys: France* (Paris, 2000), pp. 54–55.

62. See Virginie Malingre, "Le taux normal de la TVA passé de 20.6% à 19.6%," *Le Monde,* April 3, 2000.

63. Laurent Fabius, " De la nécessité de la stabcroissance," *Le Monde,* August 25, 2000. Although Fabius described his cuts as the greatest in fifty years, calculations by the Observatoire français des conjonctures économiques (OFCE) suggest that the Chirac-Balladur cuts of 1987–88 were of similar magnitude in current francs. See Virginie Malingre, "Des baisses d'impôts comparables à celles de 1987 et 1988," *Le Monde,* September 1, 2000.

64. See Fabius, "De la nécessité de la stabcroissance."

65. See Laurent Mauduit, "Le gouvernement veut des baisses d'impôts pour tous," *Le Monde,* September 1, 2000; and J. P. Morgan, "Euro Area Tax Burden Is Coming Down," *European Economic Outlook* (October–November 2000), pp. 15–18.

66. Ibid.

67. See "La conversion fiscale des socialistes," *Le Monde,* September 1, 2000.

68. See Sandrine Trouvelot, "Comment Fabius va baisser vos impôts," *Le Point,* May 31, 2000; and Laurent Mauduit, "Laurent Fabius croit possible de réduire les impôts de 170 milliards en trois ans," *Le Monde,* April 2-3, 2000, p. 7.

69. See Robert Graham, "Fabius Follows Suit," *Financial Times,* September 1, 2000, p. 16.

70. For opposition to the tax cuts on the Left, see Virginie Malingre, "Seuls les socialistes applaudissent le plan de baisse des impôts," *Le Monde,* September 2, 2000.

71. See Canal Ipsos, "Les nouvelles frontieres politiques en France," May 26, 2000 (www.canalipsos.com/articles_fr/00005/front_pol/typo.htm [June 2000]).

72. See, for example, Frédéric Denis, "Le choix de Marianne," *Le Figaro,* April 7, 2000; and Sophie Fay and Laurent Mauduit, "Start-up et grosses fortunes perdent le goût de l'expatriation fiscale," *Le Monde,* March 12, 2001.

73. See Suzanne Daley, "A French Paradox at Work: 35-Hour Week May Turn Out to Be Best for Employers," *New York Times,* November 11, 1999, p. C1.

74. See the Labor Ministry statistics in "La réduction négotiée du temps de travail au 21/05/01" (www.35h.travail.gouv.fr); and Eric Heyer and Xavier

Timbeau, "Les 35 heures," in Observatoire français des conjonctures économiques (OFCE), *L'Economie Française 2001* (Paris: Découverte, 2001), pp. 103–09.

75. See "The law on negotiated workweek reduction in France" (www.35h.travail.gouv.fr [June 19, 2001]).

76. See, for example, Robert Graham, "French MPs Pass 35-Hour Week Law," *Financial Times*, May 20, 1998, p. 2; Paul Krugman, "Is Capitalism Too Productive?" *Foreign Affairs*, vol. 76, no. 5 (1997), pp. 79–94; "Everyone Cross," *Economist*, February 5, 2000, p. 41; Ernest-Antoine Seillière (president of MEDEF), "Loi des 35 heures: la révision," *Le Figaro*, April 11, 2000; and the critiques of Denis Kessler and Philippe Trainar in "Les 35 heures et l'emploi: Illusions et effets pervers," *Commentaire*, vol. 23 (Winter 2000–01), pp. 785–98.

77. See Gunnar Trumbull, "France's 35-Hour Work Week," *US-France Analysis* (Brookings Center on the United States and France, January 2001).

78. This figure is from Commissariat Général du Plan, *Reduction du temps de travail: les enseignements de l'observation*, report of the commission presided over by Henri Rouilleault (www.plan.gouv.fr [June 2001]). If "planned" job creation or preservation (based on company planning) is taken into account, the figure rises to 357,000. See the Labor Ministry statistics at (www.35h.travail.gouv.fr).

79. With the addition of special jobs for youth (*"emplois-jeunes"*), the figure jumps to 430,000. See "French Job Growth Is Most in 3 Decades," *International Herald-Tribune*, March 11–12, 2000.

80. See Laure Belot, "Ces Entreprises qui embauchent, en France, par milliers," *Le Monde*, May 16, 2001; Isabelle Mandraud, "La baisse du chômage se poursuit au ralenti," *Le Monde*, April 28, 2001; "517,000 emplois créés en France en 2000," *Le Figaro*, February 17-18, 2001; OECD, *Economic Outlook* (Paris, 2000), p. 265; and Le Monde, *Bilan du Monde: Edition 2001* (Paris, 2001), p. 137.

81. See Patrick Jarrea, "Qu'elles créent ou non des emplois, les 35 heures changent la vie," *Le Monde*, August 16, 2000; and Daley, "A French Paradox at Work."

82. *Computer Industry Almanac* (www.c-i-a.com [June 19, 2001]).

83. See Ardagh, *France in the New Century*, p. 89.

84. *Computer Industry Almanac* (www.c-i-a.com).

85. Minitel terminals and keyboards are provided by France Télécom and allow easy access to basic information, such as train schedules and telephone numbers. Statistics on the Minitel are from (www.france.diplomatie.fr/label_france/ENGLISH/COM/AUTOROUT/autorout.html [June 2001]). Also see John Tagliabue, "France's Minitel Story, or, Pitfalls of Being a Pioneer," *International Herald-Tribune*, June 5, 2001, p. 16. On Minitel's alleged stifling of Internet use in France and on the role of English, see "Le Cyber Challenge," *Economist*, March 11, 2000, p. 36; and Geoffrey Nunberg, "Will the Internet Always Speak English?" *American Prospect*, vol. 11 (March–April 2000).

86. See Thomas L. Friedman, *The Lexus and the Olive Tree* (Farar, Strauss and Giroux, 1999), pp. 165–93.

87. In Friedman's revised paperback edition published in 2000, he acknowledged that "France is changing . . . and eventually I expect it will make an appearance on the buy list. While certain government officials and intellectuals say a lot

of silly things about and against the globalization system, French industrialists and entrepreneurs are putting on the Golden Straitjacket [that is, accepting the rewards and constraints of globalization] with a vengeance." See the updated and expanded paperback version of *The Lexus and the Olive Tree* (Anchor Books, 2000), pp. 232–33.

88. See "Le cyber challenge."

89. See Delphine Denuit, "La France creuse son retard sur l'Internet," *Le Figaro*, Section Economie, p. 1; "Internet pénètre lentement dans les foyers français," *Le Monde*, August 8, 2001; and "La ruée vers l'or du Net," *Le Monde*, March 19–20, 2000, p. 1. Also see Service des études et de Statistiques Industrielles, *L'Internet: Les François se hâtent lentement* (Paris, August 20, 2001).

90. See the report by French senator Jean-François Poncet, "Rapport d'information fait au nom de la Commission des Affairs économiques et du Plan sur l'expatriation des jeunes Français," no. 388, Sénat, Session Ordinaire de 1999–2000, p. 40.

91. See Jad Mouawad, "Internet English Challenges France's Official Translators," *International Herald-Tribune*, March 9, 2000.

92. See the CSA/*Le Parisien/Aujourd'hui en France* poll of February 28–29, 2000, published on the website of the polling firm CSA Opinion in March 18, 2000.

93. See Joseph Fitchett, "France Again Becomes an Economic Hostage," *International Herald-Tribune*, September 8, 2000, p. 2.

94. See Frédéric Lemaître, "Jean-Claude Gayssot fait d'importantes concessions aux transporteurs routiers," *Le Monde*, September 7, 2000.

95. See Tom Buerkle, "Store Closings in France Raise Storm over Jobs," *International Herald-Tribune*, April 4, 2001; and Laurent Mauduit, "Pourquoi, à tout prix, 'rendre du cash' aux actionnaires?" *Le Monde*, March 30, 2001.

96. See Isabelle Mandraud, "Gouvernement et élus s'élèvent contre les licenciements," *Le Monde*, April 4, 2001; Anne Salomon, "'Nouvelles régulations économiques': la loi fourre-tout adoptée," *Le Figaro*, May 3, 2001; Robert Graham, "Market Forces Meet French Resistance," *Financial Times*, April 10, 2001, p. 2; Robert Graham, "French Move to Double Redundancy Pay Angers Employers," *Financial Times*, April 25, 2001, p. 10; and Bruce Crumley, "Saying No to Profits," *Time*, April 23, 2001, p. 24.

97. See *OECD Economic Surveys: France*, p. 88.

98. Whereas in 1992 only 6 million French people were attracted by the idea of starting their own business, by 2000 the number had risen to 13 million. *OECD Economic Surveys: France 2000*, p. 90. Also see Pierre Lellouche, "Comment retenir les 'start-upers'"? *Le Figaro*, May 8, 2000.

99. See George Ross, "Europe Becomes French Domestic Politics," in Michael Lewis-Beck, ed., *How France Votes* (New York: Chatham House Publishers of Seven Bridges Press, 2000), pp. 87–114.

100. See Laetitia Van Eeckhout, "Une fois de plus, la réforme de l'Etat s'enlise," in Le Monde, *Bilan du Monde 2001*, p. 144; and Robert Graham, "Ambition to Be a Moderniser," *Financial Times*, February 25, 2000, p. 6.

101. See Stéphane Rozes (director of CSA Opinion), "La popularité des mouvements sociaux ne se dément pas depuis 1995," *Le Monde,* March 7, 2001.

Chapter 3

1. For a theoretical analysis of the link between culture and identity, see Michèle Lamont, "Culture and Identity," in Jonathan Turner, ed., *Handbook of Sociological Theory* (Plenum Press, forthcoming).

2. See BVA, "Impact de la mondialisation," poll taken April 5, 2000 (www.bva.fr/archives/mondialisation9940.html [June 2001]).

3. See the Sofres poll conducted in May 2000 for the French-American Foundation, "France-Etats-Unis: Regards Croisés," June 2000, p. 58 (www.sofres.com/etudes/pol/160600_france-eu.htm [June 2001]).

4. Steven Kull, "Americans on Globalization: A Study of U.S. Public Attitudes," University of Maryland, Program on International Policy Attitudes, March 28, 2000, p. 60; and Steven Kull, "Culture Wars? How Americans and Europeans View Globalization," *Brookings Review* (Fall 2001), pp. 18–21.

5. Sofres poll, "Politique et Opinion: Les valeurs et les attentes des jeunes," November 1999 (www.sofres.com/etudes/pol/231199_jeunes.html [June 2001]). Also see Ezra Suleiman, "Les nouveaux habits de l'anti-américanisme," *Le Monde,* September 29, 1999.

6. "France and World Trade: Except Us," *Economist,* October 16, 1999, p. 53.

7. See Richard Kuisel, *Seducing the French: The Dilemmas of Americanization* (University of California Press, 1993).

8. See Georges Duhamel, *America the Menace: Scenes from the Life of the Future* (Boston: Houghton Mifflin, 1931); and the discussion in Kuisel, *Seducing the French,* pp. 1–14. It is interesting to note that in the English translation of Duhamel's book, the title is much more explicit than that of the original French edition (*Scènes de la vie future*).

9. Kuisel, *Seducing the French,* pp. 1–14.

10. Cited in Kuisel, *Seducing the French,* p. 45. Gletkin was a hard-line Stalinist character in Arthur Koestler's novel *Darkness at Noon* (Macmillan, 1941), whose name came to symbolize the Soviet threat for the postwar generation in France. "Digests" refers to the *Reader's Digest,* the American publication that summarizes and excerpts books and articles and was widely read in France.

11. See Jacques Portes, "Les origines de la légende noire des accords Blum-Byrnes sur le cinéma," *Revue d'Histoire Moderne et Contemporaine* (April–June 1986), pp. 315–29; Richard Pells, *Not Like Us: How Europeans Have Loved, Hated and Transformed American Culture since World War II* (Basic Books, 1997), p. 217; and Michel Winock, "The Cold War," in Denis Lacorne, Jacques Rupnik, and Marie-France Toinet, eds., *The Rise and Fall of Anti-Americanism: A Century of French Perceptions* (Paris: Gerry Turner, 1990), p. 71.

12. Thorez's speech on April 18, 1948, is cited in Laurent Burin des Roziers, *Du cinéma au multimédia: Une brève histoire de l'exception culturelle* (Paris: Institut Français des Relations Internationales, 1998), pp. 38–39.

13. *Le Monde*, December 30, 1949, cited in Kuisel, *Seducing the French*, p. 65.

14. *Le Monde*, September 23–24, 1949, cited in Frank Costigliola, *France and the United States: The Cold Alliance since World War II* (New York: Twayne, 1992), p. 77.

15. Kuisel, *Seducing the French*, p. 17.

16. On the history of French cultural policy in the twentieth century, see Philippe Poirrier, *L'Etat et la culture en France au XXe siècle* (Paris: Le Livre de Poche, 2000).

17. See René Rémond, *Notre Siècle: 1918–88* (Paris: Fayard, 1988), p. 618; and John Ardagh, *France in the New Century* (London: Viking, 1999), pp. 482–83.

18. Maurice Duverger, "Dans la carapace d'une automobile," *L'Express*, March 5, 1964, pp. 39–40; and René Etiemble, *Parlez-vous franglais?* (Paris: Gallimard, 1964).

19. Jean-Jacques Servan-Schreiber, *Le Défi Américain* (Paris: Editions Denoel, 1967); published in English as *The American Challenge* (New York: Atheneum, 1968), quotes are from pp. 45, 192.

20. Lang's comments at a UNESCO conference on cultural policy in Mexico City in July 1982 are cited in Burin des Roziers, *Du cinéma au multimédia*, p. 77; and "Un vif incident oppose M. Lang à la délégation des Etats-Unis," *Le Monde*, July 29, 1982, p. 19.

21. See Ien Ang, *Watching Dallas: Soap Opera and the Melodramatic Imagination* (London: Meuthen, 1985), p. 2.

22. See Ardagh, *France in the New Century*, p. 429. See also Poirrier, *L'Etat et la culture en France*, pp. 160–76.

23. See Lacorne, Rupnik, and Toinet, *The Rise and Fall of Anti-Americanism*.

24. Cited in Emmanuel de Roux, "L'ouverture d'Euro Disney à Marne-la-Vallée: Pour séduire les Européens en France, les Américains ont gardé Mickey mais ont recruté Jules Verne," *Le Monde*, April 13, 1992.

25. See Richard Kuisel, "Learning to Love McDonald's, Coca-Cola, and Disneyland Paris," *Tocqueville Review*, vol. 21, no. 1 (2000), pp. 129–49.

26. See Roger Cohen, "Culture Dispute with Paris Now Snags World Accord," *New York Times*, December 8, 1993, p. C2; and Roger Cohen, "Europeans Back French Curbs on U.S. Movies," *New York Times*, December 12, 1993, sec. 1, p. 24.

27. Mitterrand is quoted by David Ellwood, "Introduction: Historical Methods and Approaches," in David Ellwood and Rob Kroes, eds., *Hollywood in Europe: Experiences of a Cultural Hegemony* (Amsterdam: VU University Press, 1994), p. 9.

28. See David Henderson, *The MAI Affair: A Story and Its Lessons* (London: Royal Institute of International Affairs, 1999). See also Edward M. Graham, *Fighting the Wrong Enemy* (Washington: Institute for International Economics, 2000).

29. See Observatoire européen de l'audiovisuel, *Statistical Yearbook 2000* (Strasbourg, 2000), p. 30.

30. Ibid., pp. 110–14.

31. See David M. Given, "Plus Ca Change, Plus C'Est la Même Chose, European Co-Production Remains Viable, for Now," *Journal of Entertainment and Sports Law*, vol. 13 (Fall 1995).

32. See *Indicateurs statistiques de la radio* (Paris: Documentation française, 1997).

33. See Ardagh, *France in the New Century,* p. 706.

34. See Burin des Roziers, *Du cinéma au multimédia,* p. 24; and "Traductions publiées en Europe" (www.quid.fr [June 2000]).

35. See Ardagh, *France in the New Century,* p. 482.

36. Observatoire européen de l'audiovisuel, *Statistical Yearbook 2000,* p. 32; and Matthew Fraser, "Europe's Asterix vs. the US Titanic," *National Post,* August 3, 1999, p. C6.

37. Burin des Roziers, *Du cinéma au multimédia,* p. 21.

38. See Centre National de la Cinématographie, "Statistiques définitives de fréquentation, Année 2000" (www.cnc.fr/d_stat/def/definitive.htm [June 2001]).

39. For statistics, see (www.culture.gouv.fr/dep/mini_chiffres). See also Alan Riding, "French Film Furor Pits Directors against Critics," *International Herald-Tribune,* December 17, 1999.

40. See Patrick Messerlin, "La politique française du cinéma: l'arbre, le maire et la médiathèque," *Commentaire,* vol. 71 (Autumn 1995).

41. See Hilary Brown, "Mon Dieu! More French Filmmakers Making Movies in English," abcnews.com, May 23, 2000.

42. The Centre National de la Cinématographie (National Cinematographic Center) uses a complex system of points (3 points for the director, 2 points for the producer, and so forth) to determine whether the film is "French" and should therefore qualify for a subsidy.

43. Commission of the European Communities, *Directive on the Coordination of Certain Provisions Laid Down by Law, Regulation or Administrative Action in Member States Concerning the Pursuit of Television Broadcasting Activities* (Brussels, October 3, 1989).

44. Ibid., art. 4.

45. Centre National de la Cinématographie (www.cnc.fr); Observatoire européen de l'audiovisuel (www.obs.coe.int); Observatoire européen de l'audiovisuel, *Statistical Yearbook 2000;* and information provided by Laurent Burin des Roziers. Also see Frédéric Martel, "France's Film Subsidy System," *Correspondence,* no. 8 (Summer–Fall 2001), p. 8.

46. See Barbara Guidice, "French Film Biz Gets Mixed Reviews," *Daily Variety,* May 12, 2000.

47. Hubert Védrine with Dominique Moïsi, *France in an Age of Globalization* (Brookings, 2001), pp. 24, 44.

48. Lang is quoted in Andrew Jack, *The French Exception* (London: Profile, 1999), p. 47; Burin des Roziers, *Du cinéma au multimédia,* pp. 28–36.

49. See Riding, "French Film Furor Pits Directors against Critics."

50. According to Védrine, this notion was suggested to him by Mexican foreign minister Rosario Green, who said that other countries would support the principle of cultural diversity. See Védrine with Moïsi, *France in an Age of Globalization,* p. 24.

51. Quoted in Poirrier, *L'Etat et la culture en France,* p. 219.

52. Védrine, *France in an Age of Globalization,* p. 22.

53. Jean-Michel Normand, "McDonald's: Critiqué mais toujours frequenté," *Le Monde,* September 24, 1999; Alain Rollat, "Vive le Roquefort libre!" *Le Monde,* September 9, 1999.

54. See, for example, Jean-Pierre Coffe, *Le Bon Vivre, le Vrai Vivre* (Paris: Best Pocket, 1991), and *De la Vache Folle en Général et de Notre Survie en Particulier* (Paris: Plon, 1999). *"La malbouffe"* is a neologism invoking the image of bad, processed, and unhealthy food (see chapter 1 above).

55. Philippe Folliot, mayor of St. Pierre-de-Trivisy, cited in Anne Swardson, "Something's Rotten in Roquefort," *Washington Post,* August 21, 1999, p. A1. Coca-Cola is not in fact the same everywhere, but Mayor Folliot would probably not be impressed by the fact that the sugar content of Coca-Cola is varied around the world.

56. Rick Fantasia, "Fast Food in France," *Theory and Society,* vol. 24 (April 1995), pp. 201–43.

57. See "French to Dine in D.C. after Disparaging US Food," Reuters, July 21, 1999.

58. Normand, "McDonald's."

59. On brasseries, see Jack, *French Exception,* p. 9; on fast food outlets, Patricia Ochs, "Tax Has Chefs Hot under Collar," *Boston Globe,* December 13, 1999, p. A4.

60. Ochs, "Tax Has Chefs Hot under Collar."

61. Andrew Jack (*French Exception,* pp. 17–18) argues that "it is in the absence of greater domestic innovation that McDonald's has done so well." For a sociological analysis of the French and fast food, see Fantasia, "Fast Food in France," pp. 201–43.

62. See Judith Valente, "The Land of Cuisine Sees Taste Besieged by Le Big Mac," *Wall Street Journal,* May 25, 1994, p. A1.

63. "Grand Angle avec René Rémond: Regard sur l'exception française," interview, *Les Echos,* October 17, 2000, p. 54.

64. See José Bové and Francois Dufour, *Le monde n'est pas une marchandise* (Paris: Editions La Découverte, 2000), p. 23.

65. See Office of Research, U.S. Department of State, "West Europeans Reluctant to Try Genetically Altered Food," *Opinion Analysis,* November 24, 1999, p. 3.

66. See Bové and Dufour, *Le monde n'est pas une marchandise,* pp. 83–84.

67. Ibid., pp. 80–81.

68. See "La résistance aux OGM s'organise," *Le Figaro,* April 17, 2001.

69. Amanda Mosle Friedman, "Let Them Eat Sandwiches," *Nation's Restaurant News,* October 11, 1999, p. 94.

70. Amy Barrett, "Hey, Why Do You Think We Call Them French Fries?" *Wall Street Journal,* December 9, 1999.

71. On the failure of U.S. companies to adapt to local cultures, see Kuisel, "Learning to Love McDonald's," pp. 129–49.

72. See Paul Cohen, "Of Linguistic Jacobinism and Cultural Balkanization," *French Politics, Culture and Society,* vol. 18 (Summer 2000), pp. 21–48.

73. See Jack, *French Exception,* p. 27.

74. See Védrine, *France in an Age of Globalization,* pp. 21, 22.

75. Cited in Dennis Ager, "Language and Power," in Gino G. Raymond, ed., *Structures of Power in Modern France* (London: Macmillan, 2000), p. 151.

76. Cited in Alan Riding, "'Mr. All-Good' of France, Battling English, Meets Defeat," *New York Times,* August 7, 1994, sec. 1, p. 6.

77. Lionel Jospin, speech to the Tenth Congress of the International Federation of French Teachers, Paris, July 21, 2000 (www.premier-ministre.gouv.fr/pm/d210700.htm [June 2001]).

78. This addition became the new article 2 of the French constitution. See Pierre Auril and Gérard Conac, *La Constitution de la République Française: Textes et Révisions,* 2d ed. (Paris: Montchrestien, 1999), pp. 10–11.

79. Gaëlle Dupont, "Après des mois de controverses, la ratification de la Charte européene au point mort," *Le Monde,* April 26, 2001; and Gérard Courtois, "La Charte des langues régionales est jugée non conforme à la Loi fondamentale par le Conseil Constitutionel," *Le Monde,* June 24, 1999.

80. See A. Szulmajster-Czelnikier, "Des Serments de Strasbourg à la loi Toubon: le français comme affaire d'état," *Regards sur l'actualité,* vol. 221 (May 1996), p. 40.

81. Jospin, speech to the Tenth Congress of the International Federation of French Teachers.

82. See Boutros Boutros-Ghali, "L'Internet en langue française," *Le Figaro,* February 26, 2000.

83. For the statement of the conference "Trois espaces linguistiques face aux défis de la mondialisation," Paris, March 20-21, 2001, see (www.francophonie.org/oif/actions/20mars.htm).

84. See Jospin, speech to the Tenth Congress of the International Federation of French Teachers.

85. See Jack, *French Exception,* p. 25.

86. See Pells, *Not Like Us,* pp. 31–32.

87. By 2001, a large majority of UN members, including former French colonies like Vietnam, had elected to receive diplomatic correspondence in English only. See Barbara Crossette, "Diplomatically, French Is a Faded Rose in an English Garden," *New York Times,* March 25, 2001, sec. 1, p. 8.

88. See Ardagh, *France in the New Century,* p. 705.

89. See Jack, *French Exception,* pp. 36–37.

90. Eight of these judgments went on to appeal and one went as far as the supreme court. See Jack, *French Exception,* p. 37.

91. See Ardagh, *France in the New Century,* p. 705.

92. Védrine, *France in an Age of Globalization,* p. 22.

93. See Hubert Védrine, "Mondialisation et Identités," speech to UNESCO, Paris, November 7, 2000.

94. For more information, see (www.culture.gouv.fr/culture/dglf [June 2001]).

95. See Jad Mouawad, "Internet English Challenges France's Official Translators," *International Herald-Tribune,* March 9, 2000.

96. See Jack, *French Exception*, pp. 42–43. For comparisons of numbers of native speakers, see Joshua A. Fishman, "The New Linguistic Order," *Foreign Policy* (Winter 1998–99), pp. 26–39.

97. See Jack, *French Exception*, p. 32.

98. See Sandrine Blanchard and Stéphanie Le Bars, "L'hégémonie de l'anglais et de l'espagnol se renforce dans les cours de langues," *Le Monde*, February 27–28, 2000.

99. See Suzanne Daley, "Pilots Just Say Non to English-Only," *New York Times*, May 23, 2000, p. A4.

100. See Arthur Isak Applbaum, "Culture, Identity, and Legitimacy," in Joseph S. Nye Jr. and John D. Donahue, eds., *Governance in a Globalizing World* (Brookings, 2000), pp. 319–29.

101. There is extensive scholarly literature on how globalization spreads and influences national cultures rather than eliminating them. See, for example, Jan Nederveen Pieterse, "Globalization as Hybridization," *International Sociology*, vol. 9 (June 1994), pp. 161–84; Arjun Appuradai, *Modernity at Large: Cultural Dimensions of Globalization* (University of Minnesota Press, 1996); Neal M. Rosendorf, "Social and Cultural Globalization: Concepts, History, and America's Role," in Nye and Donahue, *Governance in a Globalizing World*, pp. 109-34; and Applbaum, "Culture, Identity, and Legitimacy." Also see John Micklethwait and Adrian Wooldridge, *A Future Perfect: The Challenge and Hidden Promise of Globalization* (Crown, 2000), pp. 186–202.

102. Bestor uses sushi as his example: "Just because sushi is available, in some form or another, in exclusive Fifth Avenue restaurants, in baseball stadiums in Los Angeles, at airport snack carts in Amsterdam, at an apartment in Madrid (delivered by motorcycle), or in Buenos Aires, Tel Aviv, or Moscow, doesn't mean that sushi has lost its status as Japanese cultural property. Globalization doesn't necessarily homogenize cultural differences nor erase the salience of cultural labels. Quite the contrary, it grows the franchise. In the global economy of consumption, the brand equity of sushi as Japanese cultural property adds to the cachet of both the country and the cuisine." See Theodore C. Bestor, "How Sushi Went Global," *Foreign Policy* (November–December 2000), p. 61.

103. See Dominique Moïsi, "The Trouble with France," *Foreign Affairs*, vol. 77 (May–June 1998), p. 97. Also see Alain Faupin, "Comment peut-on imposer nos idées sans l'anglais?" *Le Figaro*, October 17, 2000.

104. Figures are from the OECD as cited in "Le cyber challenge," *Economist*, March 11, 2000, p. 51. Journalist Sébastien Exertier puts the French share slightly higher, at 2.8 percent, with English at 75 percent. See Sébastien Exertier, "La francophonie perdue dans la Toile," *Le Figaro*, February 21, 2000.

105. See Jeanette Borzo and Megan Doscher, "France Finds Internet Isn't Enemy," Dow Jones, December 20, 1999.

106. Reginald Dale, "Americanization Has Its Limits," *International Herald-Tribune*, January 25, 2000, p. 9.

107. See "La France demeure la première destination mondiale," *Le Monde*, February 12, 2001.

108. Jean-François Revel, "Ne craignons pas l'Amérique," *Le Point*, March 21, 1992, pp. 51–57.

Chapter 4

1. See Thierry de Montbrial, *Pour combattre les pensées uniques* (Paris: Flammarion, 2000); Helen Milner, *Resisting Protectionism: Global Industries and the Politics of International Trade* (Princeton University Press, 1988); Ronald Rogowski, *Commerce and Coalitions: How Trade Affects Domestic Political Alignments* (Princeton University Press, 1989); Robert Keohane and Helen Milner eds., *Internationalization and Domestic Politics* (Cambridge University Press, 1996); Suzanne Berger and Ronald Dore, eds., *National Diversity and Global Capitalism* (Cornell University Press, 1996); and Joseph S. Nye Jr. and John D. Donahue, eds., *Governance in a Globalizing World* (Brookings, 2000).

2. Eddy Fougier, "Les trois voix: Mondialisation, gouvernance et politique," *Accès*, July 2000.

3. See, for example, Philip Williams, *Politics in Post-War France: Parties and the Constitution in the Fourth Republic* (London: Longmans, 1958), pp. 44–140; Alfred Grosser, *La IVe République et sa politique extérieure* (Paris: Librairie Armand Colin, 1961), pp. 103–41; and René Rémond, *Notre Siècle: 1918–1988* (Paris: Fayard, 1988), pp. 397–534.

4. See Jean-Pierre Rioux, *La France de la Quatrième République*, vol. 2, *L'expansion et l'impuissance, 1952–1958* (Paris: Seuil, 1983).

5. See Olivier Duhamel, *Droit constitutionnel*, vol. 1, *Le Pouvoir politique en France* (Paris: Seuil, 1999), esp. pp. 31–73; and Olivier Duhamel, "France's New 5 Year Presidential Term," *U.S.-France Analysis* (Brookings Center on the United States and France, March 2001).

6. The PCF did agree to support Socialist leader François Mitterrand in his bid to oust de Gaulle in the 1965 presidential race, but mainly because the Communist leaders assumed, wrongly, that no leftist politician could mount a credible challenge. Mitterrand was thus able to prevent de Gaulle from getting the requisite majority in the first round, and ultimately lost by a respectable 46 percent to 54 percent in a second round of voting.

7. For a discussion of the domestic politics and geopolitical goals of the Gaullist period, see Rémond, *Notre Siècle*, pp. 615–717; and Stanley Hoffmann, *Decline or Renewal? France since the 1930s* (Viking, 1974), pp. 185–33. For an interesting revisionist assessment that puts more emphasis on the domestic political and economic factors behind de Gaulle's policies, see Andrew Moravcsik, "De Gaulle between Grain and Grandeur: The Economic Origins of French EC Policy, 1958–70," *Journal of Cold War Studies* (Spring 2000), pp. 3–34, and (Fall 2000), pp. 4–68.

8. See Valéry Giscard d'Estaing, *Démocratie Française* (Paris: Fayard, 1976).

9. See the discussion in chapter 2 above, and also Julius W. Friend, *The Long Presidency: France in the Mitterrand Years, 1981–1995* (Boulder, Colo.: Westview Press, 1998), pp. 46–112.

10. The term *pensée unique* was popularized by journalist Jean-François Kahn, first in a November 1991 article in *L'Evénement du Jeudi,* and then in Jean-François Kahn, *La Pensée Unique* (Paris: Hachette-Pluriel, 1996).

11. See François Furet, Jacques Julliard, and Pierre Rosanvallon, *La République du centre* (Paris: Pluriel, 1988).

12. See Sophie Meunier-Aitsahalia and George Ross, "Democratic Deficit or Democratic Surplus? A Reply to Andrew Moravcsik's Comments on the French Referendum," in *French Politics and Society,* vol. 11 (Winter 1993), pp. 57–69; and Annick Percheron, "Les Français et l'Europe: Acquiescement de Façade ou Adhésion Véritable?" *Revue Française de Science Politique,* vol. 41, no. 3 (1991), pp. 382–406.

13. On the Right and Maastricht, see Andrew Appleton, "The Maastricht Referendum and the Party System," in John S. T. Keeler and Martin Schain, eds., *Chirac's Challenge: Liberalization, Europeanization, and Malaise in France* (St. Martin's Press, 1996), pp. 301–24.

14. Phillipe Séguin, comment at the conference "France in Europe, Europe in France," Harvard University Center for European Studies, December 3–5, 1999. France lost the Battle of Agincourt to England in 1415, during the Hundred Years' War.

15. See "L'Euroscepticisme se concentre aujourd'hui au RPF," *Le Monde,* May 10, 2000.

16. Denis Kessler, "Les Français aiment le risque mais l'Etat les endort," *L'Expansion,* February 17–March 1, 2000.

17. The Arthuis report is discussed above, in chapter 2. See also Suzanne Berger, "Trade and Identity: The Coming Protectionism?" in Gregory Flynn, ed., *Remaking the Hexagon: The New France in the New Europe* (Boulder, Colo.: Westview Press, 1995).

18. See George Ross, "Europe Becomes French Domestic Politics," in Michael Lewis-Beck, ed., *How France Votes* (New York: Chatham House Publishers of Seven Bridges Press, 2000), p. 98.

19. Viviane Forrester, *L'Horreur Economique* (Paris: Fayard, 1996).

20. See Edward Graham, *Fighting the Wrong Enemy: Antiglobal Activists and Multinational Enterprises* (Washington: Institute for International Economics, 2000); also, Stephen J. Kobrin, "The MAI and the Clash of Globalizations," *Foreign Policy* (Fall 1998), pp. 97–108.

21. See "Lionel Jospin appelle Michelin à faire attention; le PCF souhaite plus de fermeté, la droite dénonce l'hypocrisie du gouvernement," *Le Monde,* September 13, 1999; and Martin Walker, "Jospin's Tightrope," IntellectualCapital.com, October 14, 1999.

22. See Francoise Fressoz, "Face aux bouleversements économiques, Jospin assume l'idée d'un Etat modeste," *Les Echos,* September 14, 1999.

23. See Alain Beuve-Méry and Caroline Monnot, "Les manifestations contre l'OMC ont rassemblé 20,000 à 30,000 personnes en France," *Le Monde,* November 29, 1999.

24. See Alain Minc, *www.capitalisme.fr* (Paris: Grasset, 2000), p. 219.

25. See Martin A. Schain, "The National Front and the Legislative Elections of 1997," in Lewis-Beck, *How France Votes,* p. 69.

26. Jean Viard, "José Bové, pont entre le rural et l'urbain," *Libération,* June 30, 2000.

27. See Pierre Giacometti, "La quête d'identité, au centre des nouveaux clivages politiques," Ipsos and *Figaro Magazine,* May 26, 2000 (www.canalispos.com/articles_fr/0005/front_pol/analyse.htm [June 2001]).

28. See Guy Sorman, "Eloge de la mondialisation," *Le Figaro,* February 8, 2000.

29. See Jean-Francois Revel, *La Grande Parade: Essai sur la Survie de l'Utopie Socialiste* (Paris: Plon, 2000).

30. See, for example, Minc, *www.capitalisme.fr;* de Montbrial, *Pour combattre les pensées uniques;* Elie Cohen, *La Tentation hexagonale: La Souveraineté à l'epreuve de la mondialisation* (Paris: Fayard, 1996); and Daniel Cohen, *Richesse du monde, Pauvretés des nations* (Paris: Flammarion, 1998). Also see the discussion in Erik Izraelewicz's review essay "France's New Capitalists," *Foreign Policy* (November–December 2000), pp. 88–92.

31. Jean-Marie Messier, *J6M.com: Faut-il avoir peur de la nouvelle économie?* (Paris: Hachette, 2000), pp. 20–21.

32. Quoted in "Ernest-Antoine de Seillière, boss of France's bosses," *Economist,* March 11, 2000, p. 60.

33. See "Alain Minc: accepter la banalisation . . . ," interview with Joseph Macé-Scaron, *Le Figaro,* February 14, 2001, p. 16.

34. See Isabelle Mandraud and Caroline Monnot, "Kessler égale Tocqueville," *Le Monde,* June 26, 2000.

35. See Isabelle Mandraud, "Convention d'assurance chômage: la gauche applaudit la décision de Martine Aubry," *Le Monde,* July 27, 2000.

36. See Caroline Monnot, "De nombreux dirigeants locaux du Medef se sont engagés dans la campagne municipale," *Le Monde,* March 9, 2001.

37. See Alain Madelin, "Les orphelins du marxisme perdu," *Le Figaro,* February 25, 2000; and Madelin's speech to the National Assembly, "Projet de loi relatif aux nouvelles régulations économiques," April 25, 2000 (www.demlib.com).

38. Quoted in "L'opposition contre la Bové Pride," *Le Monde,* July 2–3, 2000, p. 3.

39. See "Nouvelles régulations économiques: la droite profondément divisée," *Les Echos,* April 26, 2000.

40. "La difficile quête d'un message fédérateur," *Les Echos,* July 10, 2000, p. 6.

41. See Thierry Leterre, *La Gauche et la Peur Libérale* (Paris: Presse de Sciences Po, 2000).

42. See Giacometti, "La quête d'identité."

43. See Office of Research, U.S. Department of State, "West Europeans Tend to View Globalization Positively," European Opinion Alert, November 20, 2000; Canal Ipsos, "Mondialisation: les Français ont le trac," April 10, 2000; and CSA,

"L'attitude des Français à l'égard de José Bové et ses prises de position," poll taken June 30, 2000 (www.csa-tmo.fr/fra/dataset/data2k/opi20000629a.htm [June 2001]).

44. See "Elections législatives," May 25–June 1, 1997 (www.france2.fr/legislatives/leglega.htm [June 2001]); and Françoise Fressoz, "Legislatives: L'abstention et la dispersion des voix ont caracterisé le premier tour," *Les Echos,* May 26, 1997, p. 2.

45. See Canal Ipsos, "Elections européennes, 13 juin 1999: Le dossier de Canal Ipsos" (www. canalipsos.com/articles_fr/9905/europeennes/doss_europ.htm [June 2001]).

46. See Stanley Hoffmann, *Le Mouvement Poujade* (Paris: Librarie Armand Colin, 1956).

47. See Sophie Meunier, "France, Globalization, and Global Protectionism," Harvard University Working Paper Series 71 (February 2000).

48. For an overview of the key antiglobalization organizations in France, see Alain Beuve-Méry and Caroline Monnot, "Les anti-OMC cherchent à profiter de l'effet Seattle," *Le Monde,* December 8, 1999.

49. See Jean-Paul Besset, "Une Fièvre paysanne qui dépasse le corporatisme," *Le Monde,* September 1, 1999.

50. For the Confédération Paysanne's recent gains on the FNSEA, see Gaelle Dupont and François Grosrichard, "La FNSEA perd des voix mais préserve ses positions face à la Confédération paysanne: Le syndicat de José Bové progresse de plus de six points aux élections aux chambres d'agriculture," *Le Monde,* February 2, 2001. For a broader discussion, see Sophie Meunier, "The French Exception," *Foreign Affairs,* vol. 79 (July–August 2000), pp. 113–14.

51. Numbers supplied by the Association pour la taxation des transactions financières pour l'aide aux citoyens, May 2001. See also Sophie Roquelle, "L'irresistible ascension d'Attac," *Le Figaro*, April 30, 2001.

52. See Ignacio Ramonet, "Désarmer les marchés," *Le Monde Diplomatique* (December 1997).

53. Véronique Le Billon and Walter Bouvais, "Cette France qui dit non à la mondialisation," *L'Expansion*, October 7, 1999.

54. See Pascal Marion, "Le Diplo Attaque!" *Le Nouvel Economiste,* May 31, 2000, p. 114.

55. Interview with Susan George, Paris, December 1999.

56. See, for example, Susan George, "Alerte rouge sur le 133" (http://attac.org/fra/index.html [June 21, 2001]).

57. See Alain Beuve-Méry and Caroline Monnot, "Les anti-OMC cherchent à profiter de l'effet Seattle," *Le Monde,* December 8, 1999.

58. See Appleton, "The Maastricht Referendum and the Party System."

59. See Nicolas Weill, "L'Europe mobilise peu les intellectuels," *Le Monde,* May 29, 2000; and the MDC website (www.mdc-france.org [June 21, 2001]).

60. Christiane Chombeau, "Le RPF espère attirer les militants de droite et d'extreme droite," *Le Monde,* September 21, 1999.

61. Jean-François Revel, "Marx est mort, mais les Français ne veulent pas le savoir," *L'Expansion,* no. 618 (March 30-April 12, 2000).

62. See Alain Beuve-Mery, Cécile Chambraud, and Caroline Monnot, "Robert Hue veut faire fructifier le rassemblement du 16 octobre," *Le Monde,* October 19, 1999.

63. Quoted in Nathalie Raulin, "Des marches contre le marché mondial," *Libération,* November 29, 1999.

64. See Sofres poll data in "Une menace ou une chance?" *Le Monde,* July 19, 2001, p. 3.

65. See the section of Green Party website on employment, "L'emploi" (www.les-verts.org [June 2001]).

66. "French Group Attacks Globalization," Associated Press, April 30, 2000.

67. See "L'Extreme droite reste empetrée dans ses divisions," *Les Echos,* May 2, 2000; and "L'Epreuve de verité pour le FN et le MNR," *Le Figaro,* February 16, 2001.

68. See William Abitbol and Paul-Marie Couteaux, "Souverainisme, j'écris ton nom," *Le Monde,* September 30, 1999.

69. See Charles Pasqua, "La mondialisation n'est pas inéluctable," *Le Monde,* December 7, 1999.

70. See the commentary by Eric Dupin, "Les Limites du libéralisme français," Canal Ipsos, August 16, 1999 (www.canalipsos.com/archives_fr/0899/ nllefrance.htm [June 2001]).

71. Lionel Jospin "Mondialisation et régulations: le rôle des Etats et des organisations multilatérales," speech to the Nikkei Symposium, Tokyo, December 16, 1999 (www.france.diplomatie.fr/actual/evenements/japon/japon7.html [June 2001]). For Jospin's most comprehensive statement on globalization and French policy, see his April 6 speech to the Candido-Mendes Center and the Brazilian Center for International Relations, reprinted as "Le discours de Lionel Jospin à Rio," *Le Monde,* April 18, 2001.

72. See Lionel Jospin, *Modern Socialism,* Fabian Pamphlet 592 (London: Fabian Society, November 1999), p. 1.

73. Jacques Chirac's speech, delivered on July 14, 2000, is quoted in "La démocratie doit être rendue le plus possible aux Français," *Le Monde,* July 17, 2000.

74. Jacques Chirac, "Humaniser la mondialisation," *Le Figaro,* July 19, 2001, pp. 1, 10; Lionel Jospin, "Maîtriser la mondialisation," *Les Echos,* April 10, 2001, p. 68. Jospin's article is based on his April 6 speech in Rio de Janeiro, Brazil (see note 71 above).

75. See Keeler and Schain, *Chirac's Challenge,* pp. 1–19.

76. On the "Juppé plan" and the December 1995 strikes that forced his resignation, see Ross, "Europe Becomes French Domestic Politics," pp. 95–100; and Andrew Jack, *The French Exception* (London: Profile, 1999), pp. 165–66.

77. François Bayrou, "Pourquoi j'ai voté la taxe Tobin," *Le Point,* January 28, 1999, p. 50.

78. See John Tagliabue, "Resisting the Ugly Americans: Contempt in France for U.S. Funds and Investors," *New York Times,* January 9, 2000, sec. 3, p. 1.

79. Jospin's retort, "On n'a pas remplacé la dictature du prolétariat pour avoir celle de l'actionnariat!" is quoted in Caroline Monnot and Michel Noblecourt,

"Concurrence à gauche pour la formation d'un front anti-capitaliste," *Le Monde*, September 23, 1999. For Chirac, see Tagliabue, "Resisting the Ugly Americans."

80. See Eric Aeschimann, "Il était une foi nommée Bové," *Libération*, June 30, 2000.

81. See Judith Waintraub, "Une pierre dans le jardin de la gauche," *Le Figaro*, June 30, 2000.

82. See Ariane Chemin and Caroline Monnot, "Matignon recherche un conseiller en antimondialisation," *Le Monde*, May 24, 2001.

83. See Moisés Naïm in his interview with McDonald's CEO Jack Greenberg, "McAtlas Shrugged," *Foreign Policy* (May–June 2001), p. 26. Also see Gallaz Christophe, "Comment s'est fabriqué l'effet Bové," *Le Monde*, July 7, 2000.

84. See "M. Chirac: 'comprendre' les manifestants," *Le Monde*, July 22–23, 2001 (from which the epigraph to this chapter is taken); and "Putting the Brakes On," *Economist*, August 4, 2001, p. 43.

85. See Marie-Laetitia Bonavita, "Fabius ne la rejette plus—l'étrange engouement pour la taxe Tobin," *Le Figaro*, June 20, 2000; and Nathalie Raulin, "Taxe Tobin: Fabius passe à l'ATTAC," *Libération*, June 29, 2000.

86. See Virginie Malingre, "Lionel Jospin 'réfléchit,' de nouveau, à la taxe Tobin," *Le Monde*, July 5, 2000.

87. Speech delivered in Brazil, published as "Le discours de Lionel Jospin à Rio" (see note 71 above).

88. See "Matignon: Pas deux discours sur la mondialisation," *Le Monde*, January 25, 2001.

89. See "De Multiples appels au boycottage," *Le Monde*, April 6, 2001; Robert Graham, "Market forces meet French resistance," *Financial Times*, April 10, 2001; and Bruce Crumley, "Saying No to Profits," *Time*, April 23, 2001, p. 24.

90. See Jean-Louis Saux, "Charles Pasqua juge légitime le combat de José Bové," *Le Monde*, June 22, 2000.

91. See Dupin, "Les limites du liberalisme francais."

92. See Hervé Nathan's interview of Christophe Aguiton, "Une césure entre la gauche et le mouvement social," *Libération*, March 19, 2001.

93. Since 1997, the number of applicants to ENA has dropped by 30 percent. The number of students in the ENA preparation course at the Institut d'Etudes Politiques (Sciences Po) dropped from 1,000 in 1990 to 600 in 1995 and to 250 in 2000. See Alexandre Garcia, "La 'crise des vocations' accentue le malaise des hauts fonctionnaires," *Le Monde*, November 15, 2000; "Réforme de l'Ecole Nationale d'Administration: Enarque pour quoi faire?" *Les Echos*, January 2, 2001; and Suzanne Daley, "The Pedestal Is Cracking under an Elite in France," *New York Times*, July 9, 2000, sec. 1, p. 3.

Chapter 5

1. Conversation with Philip Gordon, Paris, October 2000.

2. Spending on social protection by European Union countries in 1997 is given in Institut National de la Statistique et des Etudes Economiques (INSEE), *Tableaux*

de l'économie française 2000/2001 (Paris, 2000), p. 101. See also Jacques Mistral, "L'heure des choix," in Roger Fauroux and Bernard Spitz, eds., *Notre Etat: Le Livre Vérité de la Fonction Publique* (Paris: Robert Laffont, 2000), pp. 307–21.

3. On health care spending, see Organization for Economic Cooperation and Development, *OECD Economic Surveys, France* (Paris, July 2000), pp. 105–32; and "Keeping Well," *Economist,* March 3, 2001, p. 31. For the WHO study, see World Health Organization, *World Health Report 2000* (www.who.int/whr/2000/en/report.htm [June 2001]); and Nicolas Timmins, "U.S. Health System Ranks Just Ahead of Cuba, Says WHO," *Financial Times,* June 21, 2000, p. 1.

4. See "No Hero He," *Economist,* March 3, 2001, p. 47.

5. Quoted in "Gouverner les forces qui sont à l'oeuvre dans la mondialisation," *Le Monde,* June 27, 2000, which provides extracts from Jospin's speech to the conference of the World Bank and the Conseil d'analyse économique, Paris, July 26, 2000. Also see Jospin's major address on globalization in Rio de Janeiro, Brazil, reprinted as "Le discours de Lionel Jospin à Rio," *Le Monde,* April 18, 2001.

6. See Lionel Jospin, *Modern Socialism,* Fabian Pamphlet 592 (London: Fabian Society, November 1999), pp. 10–11.

7. In a November 2000–January 2001 poll of over 1,600 full-time workers in firms that had adopted the thirty-five-hour work week, 59 percent of respondents said its effects "generally went in the right direction," compared with 13 percent who said it made things worse (27 percent said it made no difference). See Pascale Krémer, "La majorité des salaries jugent positif l'impact des 35 heures sur leur vie," *Le Monde,* May 14, 2001.

8. The results of the poll taken September 20–21, 1999, are published (as a chart titled "L'Etat n'intervient pas assez") in Olivier Duhamel, "Les Français et L'Etat," in Olivier Duhamel and Philippe Méchet, eds., *L'état de l'opinion 2000* (Paris: Seuil, Sofres, 2000), p. 143.

9. Chirac, speaking to supporters of the Rassemblement pour la République (RPR) on June 17, 2000, is quoted in "Je vous demande votre soutien à cette réforme," *Le Monde,* June 20, 1999.

10. "L'avenir de l'Europe: l'intégralité de l'intervention de Lionel Jospin," *Le Monde,* May 28, 2000.

11. See Lionel Jospin, "Mondialisation et régulations: le rôle des Etats et des organisations multilatérales," speech delivered at the Nikkei symposium, Tokyo, Japan, December 16, 1999 (www.premier-ministre.gouv.fr/fr/p.cfm?ref=4959&txt=1# [June 21, 2001]).

12. See Pascal Lamy, "The European Union: Between Globalization and Enlargement," speech delivered at the Dialogue on Europe, Freie Universität Berlin, February 8, 2001 (http://europea.eu.int/comm/trade/speeches_articles/spla46_en.htm [June 2001]).

13. See Sophie Meunier, "What Single Voice? European Institutions and EU-U.S. Trade Negotiations," *International Organization,* vol. 54 (Winter 2000), p. 103.

14. See John Van Oudenaren, "E Pluribus Confusio: Living with the EU's Structural Incoherence," *National Interest,* no. 65 (Fall 2001), pp. 28–29.

15. See Steven Everts, *The Impact of the Euro on Transatlantic Relations* (London: Center for European Reform, 1999); and Kathleen McNamara and Sophie Meunier, "Between National Sovereignty and International Power: What External Voice for the Euro?" unpublished paper, Princeton University, July 2001.

16. See Bové's contribution in "L'Etat doit intervenir, mais différement: Doit-on et peut-on encore réguler l'économie?" *Le Monde*, October 19, 1999.

17. See Gérard Courtois, "Les Français souhaitent un contrôle plus étroit sur les multinationales et les marchés financiers," *Le Monde*, July 19, 2001. The previous year, 38 percent said the EU "protected" France from globalization and 50 percent said the EU "reinforced" its effects; and in 1999, the figures were 45 percent and 47 percent, respectively. See Canal Ipsos, "Les Français et L'Europe," December 13, 2000 (www.canalipsos.com/articles_fr/0012/france_ue_tab.htm [June 2001]; and Canal Ipsos, "L'Europe ne protège pas assez de la mondialisation," January 27, 2000 (www.canalipsos.com/articles_fr/0001/europe_tab.htm).

18. See Canal Ipsos, "L'Europe ne protège pas assez de la mondialisation."

19. 36 percent wanted the pace of European integration to stay the same. See Canal Ipsos, "Les Français et L'Europe." A June 2000 poll asked respondents to choose only whether they wanted political and economic integration to increase or decrease: 70 percent said increase and 25 percent said decrease (5 percent did not answer). See CSA, "L'attitude des Français à l'égard de l'Europe à la veille de la présidence Française," June 26, 2000 (www.csa-tmo.fr/fra/dataset/data2k/opi20000617b.htm [June 2001]).

20. Canal Ipsos, "Les Français et L'Europe."

21. See Simon Serfaty, "The French EU Presidency and the Nice Summit: Deciding without Choosing," *U.S.-France Analysis* (Brookings Center on the United States and France, February 2001); as well as the discussion in "De la fédération à l'Europe des nations libres," *Le Monde*, May 28, 2001; and Lionel Jospin's speech, "L'avenir de l'Europe: l'intégralité de l'intervention de Lionel Jospin," *Le Monde*, May 28, 2001.

22. On EU trade policymaking, see Sophie Meunier and Kalypso Nicolaïdis, "EU Trade Policy: The 'Exclusive vs. Shared' Competence Debate," in Maria Green Cowles and Michael Smith, eds., *The State of the European Union*, vol. 5, *Risks, Reforms, Resistance or Revival?* (Oxford University Press, 2001).

23. See "L'Europe veut renforcer la régulation du commerce international," *Le Monde*, October 21, 1999.

24. See, for example, European Union, "EU Approves 'Everything but Arms' Trade Access for Least Developed Countries," press release, February 26, 2001 (http://europa.eu.int/comm/trade/miti/devel/eba3.htm [June 2001]).

25. Secrétariat général du comité interministériel pour les questions de coopération économique européenne (SGCI), "La Présidence 36: Programme" (English ed.), April 7, 2000 (www.presidence-europe.fr/pfne/static/acces5.htm [June 2001]).

26. Pascal Lamy, "Globalisation: menace ou chance pour la démocratie?" Brussels, October 26, 2000 (http://europa.eu.int/comm/trade/speeches_articles/spla20_fr.htm [June 2001]).

27. See European Commission, "Pascal Lamy Sets Out Proposals for Trade and Social Development," October 27, 2000.

28. On the EU approach, see Mario Monti, *Prospects for Transatlantic Competition Policy,* Policy Brief 01-6 (Washington: Institute for International Economics, May 2001). On the differences between the European and American approaches, see Edward M. Graham and J. David Richardson, *Competition Policies for the Global Economy* (Washington: Institute for International Economics, 1997).

29. See World Trade Organization, "United States—Tax Treatment for 'Foreign Sales Corporation': Report of the Appellate Body," WT/DS108/ABR, February 24, 2000.

30. Quoted in "L'Europe veut renforcer la régulation du commerce international."

31. The Biosafety Protocol was adopted by more than 130 countries in Montreal on January 29, 2000. For an analysis of the divergences in the regulatory approaches of the United States and the EU toward genetically modified foods, see Olivier Cadot and David Vogel, "France, the United States and the Biotechnology Dispute," *U.S.-France Analysis* (Brookings Center on the United States and France, January 2001.

32. See Sophie Meunier and Kalypso Nicolaïdis, "Trade Competence in the Nice Treaty," *ECSA Review* (European Community Studies Association), vol. 14 (Spring 2001), pp. 7–8.

33. Quoted in Roger Cohen, "Redrawing the Free Market," *New York Times,* November 14, 1998, P. B9.

34. See "Facing International Instability: Twelve Proposals for a European Initiative" (www.info-france-usa.org/news/statmnts/dsk/twelve.htm).

35. See Martine Royo and Jacques Docquiert, "Le Conseil de l'euro, qui se réunit ce soir à Vienne, examinera un memorandum français contenant douze propositions, sur la contribution de l'Union européenne à la stabilisation du système financier international," *Les Echos,* September 25, 1998, p. 5.

36. Dominique Strauss-Kahn, "Facing the International Financial Crisis: The French View," speech delivered to the National Press Club, Washington, D.C., October 5, 1998 (www.info-france-usa.org/news/statmnts/dsk/press.htm [June 21, 2001]).

37. See Babette Stern, "Douze propositions françaises pour prevenir les crises financières," *Le Monde,* September 25, 1998.

38. Hubert Védrine with Dominique Moïsi, *France in an Age of Globalization* (Brookings, 2001), p. 3.

39. Both addresses were delivered at the French Institute of International Relations (IFRI) on November 4, 1999 and later published. See Jacques Chirac, "La France dans un monde multipolaire," *Politique Etrangère* (Winter 1999–2000), p. 804; and Hubert Védrine "Le monde au tournant du siècle," *Politique Etrangère* (Winter 1999–2000), p. 819.

40. See Védrine with Moïsi, *France in an Age of Globalization,* p. 19.

41. Lionel Jospin, speech to the UN General Assembly, September 20, 1999, available as "Discours du Premier Ministre à la 54ème session de l'Assemblée Générale de l'ONU à New York" (www.premier-ministre.gouv.fr [June 2001]).

42. See North Atlantic Treaty Organization, *The Alliance's Strategic Concept,* NAC-S (99)65 (Brussels, April 24, 1999). Chirac argued that "France cannot and will not accept that a regional defense organization [NATO] designates itself as the world's gendarme, a role that is accorded by the UN Charter to the Security Council alone." Chirac, "La France dans un monde multipolaire," p. 807.

43. See Philip H. Gordon, *The Transatlantic Allies and a Changing Middle East,* Adelphi Paper 322 (London: International Institute for Strategic Studies, 1998).

44. See "Hubert Védrine juge illégaux les bombardements américains et britanniques sur l'Irak," *Le Monde,* February 21, 2001.

45. Chirac, "La France dans un monde multipolaire," p. 804.

46. Canal Ipsos, "Les Français et L'Europe."

47. See Gilles Andréani, Christoph Bertram, and Charles Grant, *Europe's Military Revolution* (London: Centre for European Reform, February 2001); and Philip H. Gordon, "Their Own Army? Making European Defense Work," *Foreign Affairs,* vol. 79 (July–August, 2000), pp. 12–17.

48. For a broader discussion of this issue, see Nicole Gnesotto, *L'Europe et la puissance* (Paris: Presses de Sciences Po, 1998).

49. See Felix G. Rohatyn, speech to the Université d'Auvergne, Clermont-Ferrand, May 12, 2000 (www.useu.be/issues/rohat0512.html [July 2001]).

Index